TEMPLE TALES

Sudha G. Tilak only takes up jobs that allow her to tell stories – tall and truthful. She has worked for over 20 years as a journalist with Indian and international publications out of Chennai, Kolkata, the UK and Delhi. Currently she works with a travel publication and lives in Gurgaon with her husband, son and imaginary pets, Posto the ginger cat and Idli the Labrador. This is her first book for children.

Praise for the Book

'*Temple Tales* is the most charming introduction to the world of the Hindu temple: brilliant in its simplicity and clarity, full of curious facts, thrilling legends and the occasional erudite snippet of art and architectural history. I wish I had had it to hand when I first introduced my own children to these wondrous cultural and spiritual treasure houses.'

– William Dalrymple

'Sudha G. Tilak's *Temple Tales* offers young readers a colourful mosaic of richly evocative and highly readable stories from temples across India, the legends and myths that hold them together and the fascinating (and often quirky) protagonists that populate this universe – all of which comes together marvellously to make a delightful read and, ultimately, a timely reminder of our vibrant cultural heritage.'

– Shashi Tharoor

SUDHA G. TILAK

TEMPLE TALES

SECRETS AND STORIES FROM INDIA'S SACRED PLACES

ILLUSTRATIONS BY SHARANYA KUNNATH

hachette INDIA

First published in 2019 by Hachette India
(Registered name: Hachette Book Publishing India Pvt. Ltd)
An Hachette UK company
www.hachetteindia.com

SRD

ISBN 978-93-88322-46-1

Hachette Book Publishing India Pvt. Ltd
4th & 5th Floors, Corporate Centre
Plot No. 94, Sector 44, Gurugram - 122003, India

Typeset in Arnhem by Manmohan Kumar, Delhi

Printed and bound in India
by Manipal Technologies Limited, Manipal

FSC
www.fsc.org
MIX
Paper | Supporting responsible forestry
FSC™ C043100

To

Aditya Biswas

my sweetest song

my brightest jewel

my rarest bloom

CONTENTS

INTRODUCTION

My earliest memory of temples goes back to Tirunelveli, the town where I was born, in southern Tamil Nadu. My grandfather's home stood in a lane sandwiched between two temples by the River Tamarabarani: the Chokkanathar (Shiva as 'the dude who slayed') Kovil, and the Vishnu temple we simply called Perumal Kovil. You could hardly ignore these two striking buildings when you stepped out of the house.

Temple visits were a huge part of my summer vacations. A visit to the Nelliappar Temple in Tirunelveli was really exciting for us kids, because it meant getting to feed puffed rice to the eager fish in the temple tank, tug at the long rope chains of the temple chariot during the festival and scramble on the temple elephant's back as it ambled down our lane. On festive nights the temple's processional deity, covered in gold and garlands, would be taken down our street for the devotees to offer worship.

Our trips to the beach were always marked by a visit to Tiruchendur's Murugan temple on the shoreline. This was followed by the teasing my dear cousin had to endure after each tonsure, as my aunt believed that shaving off the hair on his head was her best offering to the temple deity!

Then there was a visit that involved a thrilling train ride on the bridge over the Bay of Bengal and the Indian Ocean to reach the huge Ramanathaswamy Temple in Rameswaram. Another one took us to the Kanyakumari Temple, at the country's bottom-most end. I remember us kids splashing about in the cold sea water as we watched the drama at dusk, when the sun set over the sea rocks. There was also a trip that involved a breathless trek up the hill in Tiruchi to reach the Ucchi Pillaiyar Temple.

My big sister, who studied botany for a while, was the one who taught me the many names of the temple trees and flowers and provided able company in tasting the insatiable deliciousness of the laddoo from the Tirupati Balaji Temple or the *panchamritham* from Palani Temple.

Beauty Is Truth

Temples are some of the earliest forms of museums in the world, for in these sacred spaces we can see and understand the past of a region, its people, culture and traditions. They have survived for over thousands of years, holding their might over weather and war.

Those temple visits in my childhood taught me to appreciate some of the most beautiful art forms in India. Sculpture and architecture, dance and music, painting and handicrafts, decoration and design, and above all, stories of devotion and human compassion have all been associated with our temples in some way or the other.

Even today, each time I go to a temple with my mother, she unfailingly murmurs, 'Look at its beauty first!' She then points out the arch of a brow or the curve of a waist of some deity, and stares intensely at the jewellery patterns and the drape of the garments sculpted on the nymphs and goddesses on the pillars and walls (and makes sure I do too!).

While my mother made me appreciate the sights and smells of these journeys, my father filled my head with great many stories of gods and goddesses of these temples at bedtime.

He told me stories of valiant gods and celestial women and the legends around the towns, villages and forests dotted by famous temples. He took great pride in Thanjavur, the land of his ancestors, where the mighty Brihadeshwara Temple stands. As a civil engineer he marvelled aloud at the architecture and engineering skills of the ancients who built such grand structures in Thanjavur.

Did they have cement to glue the stones one on top of another to make those temple towers? I'd asked once.

No, but they had an ingenious method of interlocking the stones to build the towers up!

My father explained angles and lines in geometry through temple towers and their alignment, and arcs and parabolas through the arches of pillared halls.

He was quick to point out the irony of the large nuclear plant built in Mahabalipuram – the same town where the Pallava kings had built marvels like the Shore Temple.

Temples are treasure troves of tales from the Indian epics, the Ramayana and the Mahabharata, the *Puranas*, regional folklore and moral fables. Since the majority of the stories were narrated and spread through oral traditions, each region and its temples have their own versions of a number of familiar tales, weaved with local folklore and traditions.

The stories around temples are populated by a merry mix of gods and goddesses, mythical creatures, humans and animals. Histories of kings and queens, geography, including seashores and riverbanks, hilltops and caves, jungles and deserts are also all part of this universe.

Temple tales span a range of themes, from families and friendships, to love and hate, good and bad and devotion and doubt. Since temples are meant for prayer and worship there are also stories of piety that are moving and soulful.

While writing this book I realized that some temples are so mighty important that they have left an indelible mark on our history, culture, art and food – like the Jagannath Temple in Odisha, the Palani Murugan temple and the Brihadeshwara Temple in Tamil Nadu, the Guruyavurappan Temple in Kerala, the Shree Govindajee Temple in Manipur and many others. It's not wrong to say that these temples have shaped the traditions and culture of the regions where they are located.

A Sacred Gallery

This book is in no way a complete list of all the temples of India. It's a personal and subjective compilation of the sacred spaces that I have visited, marvelled at and read about, and wanted to share with readers, both young and old.

This book is about some of the stories, sculptures, music, dance, arts and crafts that have emerged from these places. It is a homage to those devoted men and women of another time who built and birthed wonderful art forms in these fascinating spaces.

A temple is a space to appreciate the beauty that humans can create and the devotion that can live in the human heart. So, the next time you go past a temple, visit it like you would an exhibition of the past: observe the ancient objects, listen to the tales, sample the food and marvel at the sculptures and paintings.

And if you want to sing a little prayer and talk to god within your heart, then by all means, do that too.

FOLKTALES AND LEGENDS

In India, when it comes to temples and the stories surrounding them, you can't always tell where history ends and where myth begins. You can argue for hours and hours about what's true and what's not. The easiest way to filter fact from fable is to look for proof. This proof can be in any form – sculpture, architecture, written records in literature, songs, historical documents, and so on.

But where do fables come from? Aha! Now that's a more difficult question to answer. According to some, fables come from the special capacity of humans to share stories and to embellish facts with fiction.

Most famous temples have a history behind them. There are records that tell us when they were constructed, the names of the kings who built them (who else but kings could afford to build such huge temples?), and how much it all cost.

The *actual* builders of these marvellous structures were skilled masons, stone craftsmen and, at times, soldiers of defeated armies – enslaved and taken as prisoners by the victorious kings. These soldiers were employed to carry large rocks, break stones and assist in the construction of the temples.

However, despite the records available, we know little to nothing about these invisible people, forgotten by time, whose hands built the temples. But what we do have are the stories that speak about the origins of these structures. These stories are called *Sthala Puranas*. The *Sthala Purana* of each temple is a fable or folktale that is unique to it. And these tales have existed for centuries, kept alive by the faith of the believers who visit these temples.

As you read these stories, you will notice how Shiva, Vishnu, Durga and other gods or goddesses are referred to by different names in different temples. That is so because they were named following the miracles they performed in that particular holy spot and the unique forms they took. The *Sthala Purana* of each temple details how and why these names were bestowed on them.

To listen to these temple tales is to know the richness of human imagination and the place that the art of storytelling holds in human life.

The Fight for Wisdom

Dhandayudhapani Temple, Palani, Tamil Nadu

Once, the sage Narada, the messenger of the gods and a thorough mischief-maker, decided to visit Mount Kailasha, where Shiva and Parvati lived with their sons, Muruga and Vinayaka. In the mood to play tricks as usual, Narada gave Shiva a ripe, juicy, golden mango. It was no ordinary fruit, he said, but the fruit of *gyan*, or wisdom and knowledge.

Now, Parvati wanted to cut it into two halves, so both her sons would get an equal share. But Narada stopped her, saying that the fruit *must* be eaten whole – and that it would be even better if the one who would eat the fruit only received it after completing a special task, for then it would taste sweeter.

'All right, let's have a race,' announced Shiva, calling his sons. But being gods, this was, of course, not going to be an ordinary race. Shiva told Vinayaka and Muruga that they must circle the *entire world*, and whoever did it first would receive the fruit. Excited, Muruga hopped onto his *vahana* (vehicle), a peacock, and promptly set off.

Vinayaka, however, remained where he was. He simply walked around his parents and touched their feet, asking for blessings.

'Why aren't you chasing after your brother?' asked Shiva, as he blessed Vinayaka.

Pat came his reply, 'Because *you* are my world.'

It was clear who the winner was! Parvati gave the fruit to Vinayaka for thinking out of the box and coming up with a creative solution.

Much later, a tired Muruga returned, having circled the world, and when he heard how he had been outsmarted by his brother, he left Kailasha in a huff. He chose a hilltop on Earth and, shedding his fine silks and jewels (he only wore a loincloth), stood in penance like a mendicant, holding a *dhanda* (stick).

Vinayaka, Shiva and Parvati went down to Earth to persuade him to return, but Muruga continued to sulk. Finally, Shiva looked at his son with love and said, 'You are Subrahmanya, the beloved of the learned. Why should a fruit annoy you when *you* are the fruit (*pazham nee* in Tamil) of wisdom yourself?'

From that day onwards, the town where the hill stood came to be known as Pazhani or Palani (meaning the 'fruit of wisdom') after Muruga.

Muruga, who is also known as the god of hill tribes, stands in a temple atop the Palani Hills in his monk-like fashion. The deity is prayed to as Dhandayudhapani or 'he who stands with a staff'.

The Lord of the Moon

Somnath Temple, Prabhas Patan, Gujarat

Haven't we all wondered why the moon waxes and wanes through the month? Well, there's a temple tale that tells us why. According to the *Matsya Purana*, Chandra, the moon god (also called Soma), was married to the 27 daughters of

Daksha Prajapati, who was one of Brahma's sons. Guess that turned to be quite a lot, as Chandra was particularly fond of one of his wives and neglected the others.

Understandably, that didn't play out well with the other ladies! The annoyed wives cursed him to lose all his radiance and beauty.

Soon, the nights on Earth became dark and lifeless as the moon did not shine its soft light on the lands and people below. Dull and miserable, Chandra came down to Earth to the estuary where the three holy rivers Kapila, Hiran and Saraswati joined the sea. Here, he worshipped a radiant lingam (known as *jyotirlingam*).

Shiva appeared before Chandra and said that he would not be able to reverse the curse, but he could alter it so that the moon god would go through periods of waxing and waning. He would shine brightly before slowly losing his glow, day by day, until he disappeared. Then, he would regain his glow day by day, until he went back to shining fully once again.

As the moon gained light, the town where he stood came to be known as Prabhasa or the 'well-lit place'.

The moon god received Shiva's blessing, and requested Shiva to remain in that spot as Somnath, or the lord of the moon.

The Somnath Temple stands besides the sea with a sacred *jyotirlingam* in the main shrine for worship. At night, a sound-and-light show casts brilliant colours on the temple's grand towers.

The Sacred Simian

Jakhu Hanuman Temple, Shimla, Himachal Pradesh

During the fearsome battle between Rama and Ravana in Lanka, Ravana's son Indrajit struck Rama's brother Lakshmana with a deadly arrow. An anguished Rama pleaded for help to save his brother's life. Sushena, the physician of the *vanar* (monkey) army, said that the Sanjeevni herb, found high up in the Himalayan mountains, was the only thing that could revive Lakshmana.

A distraught Rama turned to his good friend Hanuman, who swiftly flew to the Himalayas. According to a legend, Hanuman halted and rested awhile at the Jakhu Hill in Shimla on his way to the Himalayas. The hill's peak is now a flat top as a result of his massive weight! Devotees believe that it is also marked by the footprints of the awesome ape. This spot is where the Jakhu Hanuman Temple, a popular shrine in Shimla, stands.

A gigantic 108-foot statue of Hanuman near the temple overlooks the small town of Sanjauli, in the Shivalik mountains.

A Temple for the Bestie

Sudama Temple, Porbandar, Gujarat

Krishna was a special kind of divine being, for he was many things to many people. He was a darling child to his parents; a romantic hero to Radha and the *gopis*; a formidable general in war; an astute politician and protector to all those who trusted and loved him, and a great friend to boot.

Krishna's happiest days as a child were the ones he spent with his friends, especially the simple cowherds and goatherds – running amok, stealing butter, and playing pranks and games.

Sudama was one such friend and playmate. Krishna came from a royal family; Sudama was the son of a poor priest. That did not stop the two from having fun together and becoming the best of friends.

Years passed, and Krishna became the king of Dwarka. His friends were now princes and kings.

Nothing had changed for Sudama though. He had married a young woman called Niyati and had fathered many children, but he was still extremely poor.

As he wept at his misery, his wife nudged him. 'Enough of that now,' she scolded him gently. 'Why don't you ask your best friend Krishna for help?'

Sudama was horrified. 'No! He's a king. He may not even remember me from all those years ago,' he responded sharply.

'A good friend never forgets. Krishna will never turn away a friend in dire need,' Niyati said firmly, holding out a cloth bag and pushing Sudama out of the house.

'But I can't go empty-handed to see him,' sputtered Sudama.

'There's a handful of *poha* (rice flakes) knotted in a pouch in your bag; I remember you telling me how much Krishna loved to eat the snack when you were children,' she replied.

It was a blisteringly hot day as Sudama took his first reluctant steps on his long walk to Dwarka. Hungry and thirsty, he finally halted outside the palace gates. He thought the palace guards would shoo him away, for he didn't look like any friend of Krishna's.

As he stood outside, too hesitant to enter, there was a flurry of activity, and the gates were suddenly thrown open. Krishna came rushing out and enveloped Sudama in a bear hug. How had he known that his childhood friend was waiting outside to see him?

Sudama had no time to understand what was happening before Krishna dragged him into the palace, all smiles and jokes.

Krishna washed his friend's sore feet in cool, scented water. Sudama then sat down to a meal with the king himself, as Rukmini, Krishna's wife, served and fussed over him, until he burped the palace down protesting, 'My tummy is bursting!'

The friends spent the rest of the day chatting like old times, and soon, it was time for Sudama to leave.

'Oi! How have you come to meet me without my gift?' demanded Krishna.

Sudama was overcome with shame. After such a rich and hearty meal, he felt awkward about the humble gift he had brought for his friend.

'You mean your *poha*?' asked Sudama hesitantly.

Krishna greedily snatched the pouch from Sudama's bag and stuffed a fistful into his mouth.

'Oh! I've missed this so much, my friend,' he laughed, grabbing two more fistfuls. He bid his friend goodbye and said, 'Thanks for the gift – you are the best!'

Sudama started his journey back, his heart light and filled with love. As he neared his house it suddenly came back to him – the reason he had gone to Dwarka in the first place, to ask Krishna for money! He had forgotten about his difficulties amidst the laughter they had shared.

He was entering his street warily, wondering what he would tell Niyati, when he stopped in his tracks. His mud hut was missing!

Had he lost his way? He rubbed his eyes in disbelief, for in the place of his hut stood a grand mansion. He looked at it in wonderment as Niyati stepped out, dressed in the finest silks and jewels, welcoming him inside. His 24 children pranced about in their new clothes, and servants brought him water and refreshments.

'What happened...?' Sudama asked and then stopped. He knew what had happened. It was Krishna, who had known what his friend needed without him having to say it.

There is a Sudama Temple in Porbandar, Gujarat (where Sudama is said to have lived), made of white marble, a testament to this wonderful friendship. This temple, surrounded by tropical trees and plants, draws many devotees. And there is a sculpted maze in the temple complex for devotees to walk through and emerge on the other side, just like Sudama did through his many difficulties.

A Temple for the Teacher and the Pupil

Guru Drona and Ekalavya Temples, Gurugram, Haryana

Gurugram, the modern city of chrome and glass towers, has a past steeped in mythology. The city is named after Rajguru Dronacharya, the esteemed teacher of the Pandava and Kaurava princes in the Mahabharata.

Drona was no ordinary teacher. He was an expert in military warfare and weaponry, and a master battle strategist. And he had received deadly weapon kits from Parashurama, the warrior avatar of Vishnu.

In Hastinapur, Drona, who had lived a life of poverty, came to the limelight when he was spotted by the Kuru princes, who became his students in his gurukul, training in warfare. Pleased with his teaching services, King Dhritarashtra named a village Guru Gram after him.

Do teachers have favourites? Can gurus make or break students?

Well, Drona certainly did! He was very proud and possessive of the Pandava prince Arjuna, who turned out to be the best pupil he'd ever had. Drona was so won over by his dedication and excellence in archery tests and warfare exercises that he gave Arjuna special tuitions in the use of lethal weapons like the Brahmastra.

Ekalavya, a tribal youth, who had heard of Dronacharya's teaching skills, wanted admission in his school. But Drona had promised Arjuna that he would make *him* the best warrior the world had ever seen, so he said no to Ekalavya.

Not to be disheartened, the youth made a clay idol of Drona, offered his prayers in the morning and continued to practise his archery.

Upon hearing this, Drona went to see for himself and was astounded by the boy's marksmanship.

'You are the guru I hold in my heart and mind,' said Ekalavya, bowing before Drona in thanks.

'Won't you give me my fee then?' asked Drona.

'Name your guru dakshina, sir,' said Ekalavya.

'Very well. I want your right thumb,' demanded Drona.

It was a brutal request, for it meant that Ekalavya would never be a first-rate archer; and with his rival disabled, Arjuna would continue to be the topper.

Ekalavya understood the spiteful request but such was his guru bhakti that he chopped off his thumb with his knife right away and placed it at Drona's feet.

There stands a temple for the guru in Gurugram. In the shrine is a marble idol of Drona, fitted with his bow and arrows. The nearby neighbourhood has a small shrine with a tomb for the thumb of Ekalavya, the brilliant student who could not be.

The Lord of Skulls in the Land of Peacocks

Kapaleshwarar Temple, Chennai, Tamil Nadu

Brahma, the most learned of the gods, could often veer to the side of arrogance. Once, he made the mistake of being rude to Shiva, who, in a fit of fury, plucked off one of Brahma's four heads in order to strike at his pride. That head became stuck to one of Shiva's hands.

Without all his four heads, Brahma lost his powers of creation. Full of remorse, he apologized to Shiva for his haughtiness and was promptly forgiven (Shiva was known to cool down as quickly as he flared up!).

Brahma then hailed Shiva as Kapaleshwarar, or the god of his *kapal* (skull). And that's how Shiva came to be known as the lord of skulls.

A little while later, Shiva lost his temper all over again, this time at Parvati! He was explaining the meaning of the

A visit to the Kapaleshwarar Temple in Mylapore in Chennai will bring alive this legend. There is a *punnai* (Alexandrian laurel) tree in the outer perimeter of the temple, under which stands a lingam and the stone statue of a peacock that narrates the *Sthala Purana*. The brightly painted temple towers are studded with colourful sculptures of Shiva and Parvati and blue peacocks.

five sacred letters, 'Na Ma Si Va Ya' (Om Nama Shivaya), to her on Earth, when he saw that her attention seemed to be elsewhere. She was distracted by the beautiful peacocks flitting around the area, calling to the rain. Annoyed at her lack of concentration, Shiva cursed *her* to turn into a peacock and stormed out of the place.

Parvati, in the form of a peacock, found a lingam under a tree near her, and prayed to it fervently, gathering flowers with her beak to shower on the idol.

Shiva melted seeing her devotion and came down to Earth again and joined her as Kapaleshwarar. That place came to be known as Mylapore, the land of peacocks (*mylai* means peacock in Tamil).

The Shrine of Ice

Amarnath Cave Temple, Anantnag, Kashmir

Once, Shiva took Parvati to his snowy home in the Himalayas, 12,500 feet above sea level. He wanted to narrate the Amar Katha, the 'secret of the universe', to her. He chose a deep gorge in the mountains, a remote spot that no one else knew about, for the storytelling.

Since the divine secret was only for Parvati's ears, Shiva didn't take any of his other companions with him. His mount, Nandi the bull, stayed back at Pahalgam; he shook the moon goddess free from his locks at Chandanwari; he let the snakes around him slither off at Lake Sheshnag; he dropped his son Ganesha off at Mahaganesh, and performed the *tandava* or divine dance at Panchtarni to shed the earth, fire, water and air he carried in his divine being. Finally, Shiva and Parvati entered the cave.

As he narrated the story, seated on a slab of rock, a pigeon hatched from an egg beside him. It is said that the bird became immortal having heard the Amar Katha,

> Nandi is not just the mount of Shiva, but also the gatekeeper of his home. All Shiva temples have an idol of Nandi outside the shrine's doorway. Since Pahalgam is geographically the gateway to the Amarnath yatra, legends tell us that Nandi stayed back there as Shiva led Parvati up on the yatra.

and pilgrims swear they spot pigeons near this icy cave even today.

The Amarnath Cave is a huge glacial temple set in an enormous cave over 130 feet in height. In this icy shrine is a large stalagmite in the shape of a mammoth lingam. Pilgrims undertake this long and dangerous trek each year to behold this sacred stalagmite and seek the secret of the eternal truth that Shiva (or Amarnath) once told Parvati.

Lord of Land's End

Ramanathaswamy Temple, Rameswaram, Tamil Nadu

After days and days of fighting, Rama finally slew Ravana in Lanka. Amidst much fanfare, he and his victorious army made their way back to India. However, Rama's friends warned him that Shiva was quite upset with him, as Ravana had been a staunch devotee of the god. Rama had to do something quickly to appease Shiva.

So there, at the bottom-most tip of India, Rama stoked a fire for a yagna and sent his trusted aide Hanuman to fetch a lingam from Mount Kailasha.

Unfortunately, Hanuman could not return in time for the ritual prayers. Rama did not want to miss the auspicious time to perform the puja, so he asked Sita to fashion a lingam from the sand on the beach. This makeshift idol was called Ramalingam.

As the puja drew to an end, a flustered Hanuman returned with a lingam made of crystal – a shiny stone called Vishwalingam. Disappointed that Rama didn't use the lingam that *he* had brought, Hanuman tried to crush the Ramalingam with his tail. It was made of sand after all, so it should have crumbled in a second. But, no matter how hard he hit it with his tail, the lingam simply did not crumble!

Finally, Rama calmed the petulant Hanuman down, saying that although a temple would be built in that place for the Ramalingam, devotees would have to pray *first* to the Vishwalingam. That place is known as Rameswaram today.

The Ramanathaswamy Temple is a huge structure, dotted with 53 *theerthams*, or holy water tanks, for devotees to take a dip, and long temple corridors with over a 1,000 pillars!

Goddess of Cool

Sheetala Mata Temple, Gurugram, Haryana

Sage Katyayan was a devotee of the supreme goddess, Durga. He felt that she had to arrive on Earth as a warrior to fight the evil demons destroying its peace. So, he performed a yagna to invoke the goddess. Pleased with his devotion, she arrived on Earth in the form of his daughter, the beautiful Katyayani.

Little Katyayani had many playmates. Once, a demon called Jwarasu or the 'Fevered One' struck many of her little friends with poxes, cholera, sores and other fevers. To fight this, Katyayani assumed the avatar of Sheetala

Devi or the goddess of warding off fevers, who would cool down the body (*sheetala* means cool).

Armed with a short broom, a fan, a jar of pulses (indicative of poxes) and a cup of water, seated atop a donkey (a beast of burden in many regions of north India), she helped cool down the fevered bodies of the children. Today, there are many Sheetala Mata temples across north India.

Devotees offer cold food or food made the previous day to the goddess, instead of steaming-hot rice or sweet puddings, as prasad. At the Sheetala Mata Temple in Gurgaon, the deity takes the form of Kripi, an avatar of the wife of Guru Dronacharya.

The God Who Is Half Woman

Ardhanareshwara Temple, Tiruchengode, Tamil Nadu

Amidst the dusty shrub land of north-west Tamil Nadu rises a towering hill that has a red rock face. The hill's colour was the result of a bloody battle between Vayu, the wind god, and Adisesha, Vishnu's celestial serpent, to prove who was the strongest.

Vayu blew with all his might, and the giant serpent Adisesha, who was wrapped around Mount Meru, snapped and flew far away in the wind, landing on a hill, splattering blood all over it. Hence, the hill came to be called Tiruchengodu or the 'sacred hill streaked with red'.

There is a stunning temple with grand sculptures atop this hill. In the shrine stands a rare form of Shiva, as Ardhanareshwara or Ammaiappan or 'mother and father'. Ardhanareshwara is Shiva and Shakti fused into one deity.

According to legend, Sage Bhringi, a fierce devotee of Shiva, once visited Mount Kailasha to pay his respects to the god. Now Nandi suggested that Bhringi pay his respects to Parvati before meeting Shiva. But Bhringi just walked in and, ignoring Shakti nearby, attempted to circumambulate (go around) his *eshwar* (god). A cross Shakti hopped onto Shiva's lap, saying that Shiva and Shakti were not different but the two halves of the universe's energy. One did not exist without the other!

Bhringi, petulant as ever, tried to transform himself into a bee and buzz his way between Shiva and Shakti.

That was it! Irritated by his silly behaviour, Shakti sucked the flesh out of his body.

Bhringi turned into skin and bones, like a balloon without air! Without flesh to support his body, he collapsed pretty quickly, and Shiva, sorry for his devotee, gave him a third leg. He then performed a miracle before Bhringi by fusing half his body with half of Shakti's and appeared in the form of Ardhanareshwara.

A chastised Bhringi left hopping on his third leg after this, but Parvati now felt bad about losing her temper and decided to do penance. She chose the hill of Tiruchengode and prayed to Shiva for a long, long time.

Shiva was so pleased with her that he told her she could ask him for whatever she wanted. Parvati smiled and said that she wanted the two of them to be inseparable. So to worship her was to worship him, and vice versa, and nobody had to worry about who came first!

And that is why there is a temple on this hill dedicated to this special form of Shiva and Parvati, the Ardhanareshwara, or the half-man, half-woman form of God.

Born of Gods

Sabarimala Ayyappan Temple, Pathanamthitta, Kerala

Along the green, undulating hills of the Western Ghats, on the banks of the River Pamba, is the holy pilgrim town of Sabarimala.

According to the Ramayana, Rama, while he was journeying through the forests in search of Sita, met an old tribal woman called Sabari, who lived in the foothills of the Western Ghats and whose devotion touched his heart.

Rama ate the berries that Sabari lovingly fed him, and blessed the hillock to be named after her. Now, one of the most famous temples in south India stands here, located in a forested sanctuary called the Periyar Tiger Reserve.

It is a temple dedicated to Ayyappan, the god who sits in the ascetic pose, worshipped ardently by his devotees.

Once, the demoness Mahishi was wreaking havoc on the people who lived in the mountains. She wanted revenge, for Goddess Durga had killed her brother, Mahishasura. She undertook an intense penance and secured a boon from the gods that no being born of a man and woman could kill her.

The people of Sabarimala prayed for help, and Shiva and Vishnu met here to produce a divine being. Since Mahishi had made sure no being born of a man and woman could harm her, Vishnu turned into a celestial woman named Mohini, and married Shiva. They had a beautiful baby boy, whom they left in the forests of Sabarimala.

They knew that King Rajashekara, a devotee of Shiva, was hunting in the forest. The king did not have any children, and had been praying to Shiva desperately for a child for many years. And right there in the jungle, King Rajashekara saw what he had always wanted. Unafraid of the wilderness surrounding him, an infant lay on the ground, wrapped in silk, wearing a glittering gem necklace.

The overjoyed king picked up the baby and named him Manikandan, meaning 'he who is adorned with gems'. He took him to the palace, where the royal couple brought up the child as their own.

Manikandan was a kind and caring prince, and the king groomed him to be a fearless warrior, who would be fully prepared to take the throne when the time was right.

Meanwhile, the queen was blessed with another son. One of the king's ministers, an evil man, convinced the queen that Manikandan would throw her and her son out of the palace once he became king, and that the only way to ensure their safety was to kill Manikandan.

The queen then lay in bed, groaning and moaning, acting as if she was gravely ill. The minister told the king that only a drink made of a tigress's milk would cure the queen of her unnamed fever.

Seeing the king's sorrow and the queen in pain, Manikandan, then only 12 years old, offered to go to the forest and bring back milk from a tigress, despite his father's protestations.

Manikandan knew that this was the forest where the demoness Mahishi lived. He used the opportunity to fulfil his destiny and destroy Mahishi.

Manikandan was a mere slip of a boy, but he was the divine miracle created by Shiva and Vishnu, and hence could break Mahishi's boon and slay her. Mission complete,

Shiva and Vishnu appeared in the forest and asked him to return to heaven with them. Manikandan, however, said that he wanted to fulfil the promise he'd made to King Rajashekara. At that time, Indra, the lord of the heavens, and his *devaloka sundaris* (heavenly female beings) decided to help. They turned into tigers and tigresses to accompany Manikandan back to the kingdom.

As King Rajashekara waited anxiously at the gates of the palace, the evil minister and the queen by his side, they beheld an extraordinary sight. It was Manikandan, sitting astride a tiger, surrounded by many tigresses, walking towards them.

Sensing his divine presence, the queen wept and begged for forgiveness. King Rajashekara was overjoyed to learn that Manikandan had been created by the god he worshipped, Shiva.

When Manikandan said he would return to the heavens as his task of killing Mahishi was complete, Rajashekara pleaded with him to stay back and bless the kingdom.

Manikandan was unable to refuse his dear father, so he transformed into the deity Ayyappan. The king built a temple in Sabarimala for Ayyappan, and this remains a powerful pilgrim destination in south India.

The Horse-God of Learning

Devanathaswamy Temple, Thiruvanthipuram, Tamil Nadu

In the Devanathaswamy Temple in Tamil Nadu, it is not odd to find students placing their textbooks, notebooks and even pens before the shrine of Lord Hayagriva, the half-man, half-horse form of Vishnu. That's because Hayagriva is considered to be the god of education and learning.

Once, two wicked demons called Madhu and Kaitaba, better known as Ignorance and Temper, pinched the Vedas from under Brahma's nose and fled to Earth. A distraught Brahma went to Vishnu and sought his help, as the world would plunge into illiteracy without the wisdom of the Vedas.

So, Vishnu took the form of a man with the face of a horse and galloped to Earth, chasing the two knowledge-stealers. (Horses are not just known for their speed and strength, but also for their innate intelligence.) In that form, Vishnu was known as Hayagriva or 'he of the horse's neck', clothed in white, the colour of intellect. He found the two demons and destroyed them, returning the Vedas to Brahma. The battle symbolized the victory of intellect over ignorance.

While many Vishnu temples do have shrines for Hayagriva, the Devanathaswamy Temple is special, as it is believed that Hayagriva imparts knowledge to those who pray here for a good education.

The Dumbstruck Demon

Mookambika Temple, Kollur, Karnataka

Sage Kola, after whom the town of Kollur is named, was a devotee of Shiva. Now, in the Kollur area, there lived a demon named Mooka, who found great pleasure in destroying the peace of innocent people. The asura had received a boon from the gods. He could not be destroyed by men on Earth or even the gods in heaven. So, Sage Kola prayed to the mother goddess Ambika to vanquish the evil demon.

Hearing that Kola was plotting to render him powerless, the demon began his own penance, to ask the gods for another boon to protect himself. The gods arrived, but so did Ambika, who promptly struck the demon dumb, so that he could not utter his wishes aloud!

People then began to call him Kumbha Mookasura or the Dumb Demon. Angry about being outwitted, the demon began to terrorize the people around him even more. Finally, Ambika killed him in a bloody battle.

As he lay dying, a wave of remorse swept over Mooka and, as his final wish, he begged the mother goddess for forgiveness. Ambika not only forgave him, but also agreed to stay on in Kollur as the mother of Mooka (Mookambika).

The deity in the temple is seated on a lotus and has four arms. One hand holds the conch, to signal war, and the other, a discus, a weapon to destroy. Her other two hands offer boons and protection to devotees.

A Lesson for Shiva

Swaminathaswamy Temple, Swamimalai, Tamil Nadu

One day, Shiva asked his son Muruga if he knew the meaning of 'om', the first cosmic sound in the world.

Muruga replied he would answer such a deep question only if Shiva shed his ego, for pride always comes in the way of learning.

Shiva understood and followed Muruga, who led his father to a hillock in a forest. Once they reached the top, Shiva knelt before Muruga, much like a disciple before his guru or swami and bowed his head to receive the wisdom that his son was going to share. Hence, the spot was called Swamimalai, or the Hill of Swami, and the deity in the temple is Muruga, standing tall, as Swaminathan or the 'mentor of Shiva'.

At the bottom of the hill is a shrine for Shiva as a lingam, reminding followers of this legend.

According to Tamil Sangam literature, Earth is composed of five landscapes – hills, forests, coasts, plains and deserts. Kurunji was the hilly land and Muruga was lord of the hills, the home of the hunting tribes, nomads and gypsies. All the six abodes of Muruga in Tamil Nadu are located on hilltops.

The Divine Drama

Jagannath Temple, Puri, Odisha

The city of Puri in Odisha looks like a conch from above, which is why it's also called Sankha Kshetra. It is most famous for its magnificent temple for Jagannath, the lord of the universe.

Long, long ago, Puri was a wooded area, filled with neem trees. Indradyumna, the ruler of the kingdom, was a devotee of Lord Vishnu. One day, he learnt that a tribal chief called Viswavasu, who lived deep in the forest, apparently worshipped a powerful deity called Neela Madhava.

Intrigued, the king sent his trusted assistant, Vidyapati, to meet the tribal chief and find out more about the deity. But Viswavasu refused to share any information, so Vidyapati secretly followed him to a dark cave, dropping mustard seeds along the way to mark the path back.

A few days later, Vidyapati took King Indradyumna with him for a darshan of Neela Madhava, by following the trail of mustard plants that had sprouted from the seeds. However, when the king peered inside the cave, he found it empty.

Crestfallen, he returned to his palace. That night, he had a dream in which Vishnu came to him and said he would like a temple built in his name, and that the deity should be made of fragrant wood.

The king walked to the seashore to meditate so he could think about how to make this idol for the temple. Miraculously, he found a log – twinkling as bright as a *nilamani* (blue gem) – floating on the waves.

As the king was appreciating the radiance of the log, an old man mysteriously appeared and offered to make an idol using that piece of wood. An idol that would befit the status of being placed in a powerful temple! His only condition was that he should be allowed to work in absolute secrecy, and that nobody could see the idol until it was completed.

On the fourteenth day, unable to bear the suspense any longer, King Indradyumna's queen pushed open the door of the old man's workshop to take a quick peek. It turned out that the old man was none other than Biswakarma, the architect of the gods! Furious that his words had not been heeded, he disappeared, leaving behind the half-sculpted idols of Lord Jagannath, his sister, Subhadra, and his brother, Balabhadra.

Even now, eons after the Jagannath Temple was built, the idols are regularly sculpted out of fresh neem wood, painted and placed inside the sanctum to resemble the ones that the angry Biswakarma had left half-finished.

> The word 'juggernaut' means a massive force that is virtually unstoppable. The word's origins point to the Jagannath Temple, as its gigantic *rath* resembles a giant vehicle rolling down the road.

The Sacred Flame

Arunachaleshwar Temple, Thiruvannamalai, Tamil Nadu

Brahma and Vishnu once had a huge argument over who was the superior god. Finally, they called upon Shiva to decide the matter once and for all. Shiva gave them a task: one of them had to find the crown of Shiva's head way up above the clouds and the other had to find Shiva's feet, well into the bowels of the earth. Whoever completed this task would be considered the superior and the winner of the challenge.

Brahma swiftly flew up to see Shiva's head while Vishnu dove down to see his feet. Halfway down his journey, Vishnu realized that Shiva's form was endless and that it could not be measured, so he accepted defeat. Brahma's pride, however, did not allow him to do the same. He continued on his journey. As he was flying up, he saw a *ketaki* flower falling off Shiva's matted locks. Realizing the futility of his task, Brahma asked the flower to lie on his behalf and say that he had indeed seen the top of Shiva's head.

Shiva, furious at Brahma's lie, transformed himself into a burning column of light atop a hill called Arunagiri. This was a sacred red hill in Thiruvannamalai. The flaming pillar was so mighty, it seemed to light up the entire universe, burning evil and ending darkness in hearts and minds.

That day is celebrated as Maha Shivaratri in the country, when thousands of lamps are lit at the Thiruvannamalai Hill. At the top of the hill is a burning flame inside a temple. Here, Shiva is worshipped as the god of fire or Agni.

The Trouble with Saturn

Shanieshwaran Temple, Thirunallar, Tamil Nadu

Of all the nine planetary deities, there is none more feared than Saturn, the dark lord of Saturdays. Shani was the only offspring of the Sun, god of light, and his wife, Chaaya, the goddess of the shadows.

Shani was a very serious god. He was dark, lame in one leg, wore only black, liked the bitter black sesame, and was often known to bring misfortune with him when he visited a person's astrological house.

Though just and generous at times, Shani was known to create difficulties for the gods in heaven as well as people on Earth. So it wasn't surprising that everyone was as scared of him as they were of Shiva, known for his fearsome temper.

It was at Thirunallar that the two fearsome gods had a face-off over a devotee.

A long time ago, there was a forested region called Darbaranyam (*darba* means grass, and *aranyam* means forest). It was overgrown with *darba,* a tropical grass often used in Vedic rituals and for worship. There was a temple in that region for Shiva, who was called Darbaranyeshwar.

The king of that region, Nala, was an ardent devotee of Shiva, and prayed to him in this temple. Nala had a happy life – a loving wife, lovely children and a prosperous kingdom. He loved the arts and was even a fine cook.

It is believed that all the nine planets pass through people's lives at different points in time. Each planet has a particular effect on the person's life at that time. When Shani visits a person's astrological space, it is called Shani *dosha* and it can last for either seven or twelve years. And those years are supposed to be full of struggles.

Now it was time for Shani, as per his planetary timetable, to pay a visit to King Nala's astrological house. But Nala was under Shiva's protection, much to Shani's dismay.

One day, Nala faltered in his prayers; he did not stand in the correct posture while praying. Shani, bitter about his own lameness, was known to hurt people in the leg during their Shani *dosha*. This time, too, he took advantage of Nala's careless posture while praying by clinging to his leg and scaling up his astrological chart. Trials and misfortunes

The Planet Temples of Tamil Nadu

The nine planet gods are Surya (Sun), Sukran (Venus), Thingal (Moon), Sevvai (Mars), Budhan (Mercury), Guru (Jupiter), Shani (Saturn) and Rahu and Ketu (the twin planets who criss-cross the Sun and the Moon's path), each with their own legend.

The Chola kings were the first to build temples for the nine planetary gods (7–12th century CE) in one place in Tamil Nadu. The temples are in nine villages in and around Kumbakonam, a town in Thanjavur.

Once the Sage Kalava prayed to the gods to cure his illness. The nine planet gods took pity on him and granted his request. But Brahma was not too pleased. He said the planets could not aspire to be gods and offer boons to humans. He cursed them to go to Earth and suffer from leprosy. The planets did penance and prayed to Lord Shiva, who cured them and said the spot where they did their penance would belong to them. He bestowed upon each of them the status of a powerful deity. Hence nine temples for the nine planet gods sprung up around Kumbakonam. As a mark of respect, the presiding deity in all nine temples remains Shiva.

rained down on Nala. But Nala prayed and prayed and then prayed some more to Shiva and took a dip in the holy pond by this temple to wash away his bad luck. Finally Shani, moved by his devotion, left Nala's astrological house and restored his family, kingdom and fame.

Shiva admired Shani's determination to pass through the astrological houses of all people, good or bad, without partiality, as in the case of Nala, and offered him the most important space in this sacred temple at Thirunallar (the word means 'the sacred pond of Nala's healing').

On Saturdays, this temple is filled with devotees, who beseech Shanieshwaran to alleviate their sufferings by lighting clay lamps filled with sesame oil.

In Sleeping Splendour

Anantha Padmanabhaswamy Temple, Thiruvananthapuram, Kerala

Once upon a time, a pious man named Vilwamangalathu Swami lived on Earth and performed a severe penance for Lord Vishnu. Pleased with his devotion, Vishnu appeared before him, and blessed him with a little boy who would always give him company.

The boy, however, was very naughty. One day, he tried to distract the swami when he sat down to pray by swallowing a divine pebble called *saligram*, which had been kept aside for worship. Vilwamangalathu Swami scolded the boy and pushed him in a fit of rage. The boy got up calmly and said, 'If you want to see me again, find me at Anantha.'

That's when the swami understood that the little boy was none other than Vishnu! He immediately left in search of the god.

The swami's search took him all over Kerala. Finally, he found an old tribal woman, who pointed him to the Anantha forest. Vilwamangalathu Swami ran into the forest, calling the god's name, only to find a gigantic *illupa*, an Indian butter tree, blocking his way.

The swami begged Vishnu for forgiveness, and asked the god to make himself easier to see. Vishnu obliged and shrunk himself to a form that came to be known as Anantha Padmanabhaswamy ('the one who reclined in his serpent bed in the Anantha forest').

The king of the region heard of this miracle and built a temple for Anantha Padmanabhaswamy.

The Divine Boy of Miracles

Guruvayurappan Temple, Guruvayur, Kerala

When Krishna left his human form in Dwarka, in Gujarat, to go back to the heavens, he left a symbol of his Vishnu avatar behind. It was an idol that was given for safekeeping to his devotee Uddhava.

One day, Dwarka was flooded by a mighty storm, and the swollen sea swept away the idol. Uddhava cried for help to protect the deity. Luckily, his cries were heard by the god Brihaspati, also called Guru, and Vayu, the wind god. Guru and Vayu managed to save the idol from the roaring sea and travelled with Uddhava to Kerala.

Here, Guru and Vayu set the idol down by a beautiful lotus pond and built a shrine around it. The spot came to be called Guruvayur after them. The god in the temple is called Guruvayurappan, and stands in the form of Vishnu with the baby-faced charm of Krishna. His arms at the back hold aloft a conch and discus, the symbols of Vishnu, while his hands in front hold a flute and a pot of butter, symbolizing Krishna.

The Debt of Love

Balaji Venkateswara Temple, Tirupati, Andhra Pradesh

A sage is a person full of wisdom and learning. Our temple legends tell us that they were humans first and then sagacious. Most of them, however, were quick to lose their temper, for the silliest reasons.

Take the story of Rishi Bhrigu, for example. Now he was a sage famous for his impatience. One day, he decided to visit Vaikuntam, the abode of Vishnu.

When he trotted in uninvited, he found Vishnu and Lakshmi, the goddess of prosperity, reclining on Adisesha, their serpent bed, unmindful of the great sage's presence.

Bhrigu, all huffed and puffed from his journey, was annoyed that the divine duo were resting in their own house without a care for their guest! Not one to mind his manners, Bhrigu kicked Vishnu in the chest to stir him.

Now Vishnu had the divine presence of mind to understand Bhrigu's ill temper. Instead of getting angry,

Vishnu merely calmed the sage down by offering him a seat and then proceeding to massage his foot, which was surely aching from the kick!

Bhrigu was pleased and left the place feeling a little remorseful. To make amends, he returned to Earth and praised Vishnu as the kindest of gods to all the sages.

Back in Vaikuntam, the entire episode had greatly upset Lakshmi, as the sage had kicked Vishnu in the chest, the spot in his heart where *she* resided. Hurt and angry, she left Vaikuntam to go to Earth.

A saddened Vishnu went in search of his beloved Lakshmi near the Venkatadri Hill in the guise of a young man called Srinivasa, and began a long penance by an anthill.

A cow, sensing a divine presence, began to stand over the anthill and shed its milk over the meditating Srinivasa. The cowherd, angry that his cow was giving all her milk to this strange man instead of his farm, took his axe and swung it at Srinivasa. Unshaken, Srinivasa started bleeding from his scalp. Nothing could interrupt his meditation. A local princess, who happened to be nearby, ran to Srinivasa's rescue and stopped the bleeding by covering his scalp with her hair. (Even today, many devotees offer their hair at the temple.)

A little later, the princess, Padmavati, was walking through the woods when the sight of a wild elephant frightened her. Hearing her cry for help, Srinivasa finally emerged from his penance and rescued her. Her grateful father, the king, offered her hand in marriage to Srinivasa, who happily agreed, but quickly realized that he didn't have any money for the wedding! So, he took a loan from none other than Kubera, the god of riches himself. (It is said that the Tirupati Temple is the richest in the world as all the money offered by the devotees is helping Srinivasa pay back his huge wedding loan!)

When Lakshmi heard that her beloved Vishnu had remarried on Earth, she immediately came to the Tirupati shrine and took up residence in his heart once again. Srinivasa turned back into Vishnu, and assumed the form of a large, black granite deity. On his heart, there are two sculpted forms – Padmavati Devi on his right, and Lakshmi on the left.

Sacred Rodents

Karni Mata Temple, Deshnok, Rajasthan

Once upon a time, there lived a woman named Karni, a respected figure from the Charan community in Rajasthan. She was believed to be an avatar of the mother goddess Parvati and hence, even when she was 150 years old, she remained youthful and radiant. Kings and commoners alike would seek her blessings.

One day, her son Lakshman was drinking water in a nearby pond, when he fell in and drowned. A shattered Karni Mata beseeched Yama, the lord of death, to revive her son.

Yama could take life, but not give it back. However, he was moved by the pleas of Karni Mata, so he reincarnated her son as a rodent. Locals believe that Lakshman, Karni

Mata and all her other sons were reborn as rats after their deaths.

Devotees place sweets and milk as offerings to the thousands of black rats that live in the Karni Mata temple (also called the Rat Temple) in Deshnok, near Bikaner in Rajasthan. Over here, people tread carefully, making sure they do not accidentally step on or hurt the rats scurrying around.

The sighting or darshan of a few white rodents among the thousands of black rats is considered particularly auspicious. Even today, the Charan people revere these rats as their holy ancestors and pray for their well-being.

Temple of the Lion God

Varaha Lakshmi Narasimha Temple, Simhachalam, Andhra Pradesh

Inside this grand and ancient temple, filled with ornamental sculptures, is a shrine for Varaha Lakshmi Narasimha, a unique deity that is half-human and half-lion. Located on a hill near the Ratnagiri forests, the sea breeze from the coast is said to whip around the deity to cool its anger, for Lord Narasimha was still hot with anger when the temple was built.

The demon Hiranyakashipu had wreaked havoc in his kingdom by punishing all those who prayed to Vishnu. Now, the demon had received a boon from the gods, as a result of his many years of penance deep in the forests.

No human, man or woman, could kill him. He would meet his end neither inside nor outside, neither during the day nor at night, and neither in the sky nor on the ground. Phew, that pretty much covered everything! Which is why Hiranyakashipu was convinced that nobody could ever defeat him, and he could terrorize anyone he wished without fear of any consequences.

Hiranyakashipu's son, Prahalada, however, was completely different. He refused to stop praying to Vishnu like his father commanded. Fed up of his own son's wilfulness, the demon king flew into a rage, and tied Prahalada up and threw him into the sea and placed a mountain, the Simhadri, on top of him!

But the boy survived. Vishnu saved him and left him ashore, unharmed.

An annoyed Hiranyakashipu dragged the boy home from the seafront, so he could get rid of him properly this time. He asked Prahalada where his god Vishnu was to be found. Prahalada answered that Vishnu was everywhere to protect his believers.

Hiranyakashipu angrily kicked a mighty pillar in his palace, asking if Vishnu was in that. Lo and behold! The pillar cracked open and Vishnu emerged in his Narasimha avatar. He was neither man nor beast, but half-lion and half-human. It was dusk then, so it was neither day nor night. With a fierce roar, he dug his large claws into Hiranyakashipu's belly, and seating himself on the verandah, neither indoors nor outdoors, he mauled the demon to death.

The temple at Simhachalam is located strategically, to allow the sea breeze to cool the god's anger. The idol is always covered in sandalwood paste in yet *another* attempt to reduce Narasimha's white-hot rage!

The Lord of Beginnings

Girijatmaj Ganapati Cave Temple, Junnar, Maharashtra

Maharashtra is famous for its temples dedicated to Ganapati. Each one of them is special, but none is as unique as the Girijatmaj Ganapati Cave Temple.

Ganesha, or Ganapati Bappa, as they call him in Maharashtra, is a beloved god. Once, Shiva was away with his *bhoota ganas*, his attendants, in the forests, and Parvati was alone. As she sat down to have her bath, she moodily played with the scented body clay, or *ubtan*, used for scrubbing and bathing, and formed the figure of a beautiful boy. Marvelling at her own creation, she infused life into the form.

After spending hours playing with him, a tired Parvati asked the boy to guard the doors of her chambers and went to rest, as she did not want to be disturbed during her nap. When Shiva returned, he found the doors locked, blocked by a radiant lad who refused to let him in, as his mother was resting and could not be disturbed!

An angry Shiva lopped off the boy's head and pushed his way inside. Hearing the commotion, Parvati woke up and was horrified to see her beloved son slain by Shiva.

Ashamed of his temper and eager to calm the sobbing Parvati, Shiva summoned his fierce companions, the *bhoota ganas*, and told them to rush into the forests and return with the head of the first animal they could hunt down.

As they hurried into the forests, the *ganas* beheld an elephant, a handsome creature known for its keen intelligence. They rushed back with the elephant's head, and Shiva fused it with the boy's body and blessed it to come to life. Shiva named the boy Ganesha, or the lord of the *ganas*.

Parvati was overjoyed to see her chubby Ganesha alive again. Shiva showered him with blessings, saying that Ganesha would be the first god people prayed to in all temples. He would be the lord of good beginnings, the remover of obstacles, and the wise and intelligent one.

At Lenyadri (cave mountains in Maharashtra), there are 18 unusual Buddhist cave temples. The eighth cave is dedicated to Lord Girijatmaj, a Ganesha deity, carved on the rock face, covered in orange vermilion and worshipped by devotees.

According to the folklore here, Girija is another name for Parvati, the daughter of the mountains, whose son Ganesha defeated the evil demon Sindhu at Lenyadri.

Divine Games

Shrinathji Temple, Nathdwara, Rajasthan

There was once a princess, Ajab Kunvari, in Mewar, who loved playing board games. She found a fun playmate in a little boy, Shrinath, who would come daily to her haveli, to play her favourite board game, the *chaupar*. Little did she know that Shrinath was Krishna himself!

Each time Shrinath left her palace for Govardhan, his home, after the game, Ajab Kunvari would throw a tantrum. She wanted her dear friend to stay with her forever. Shrinath promised her that when the time was right, he would move to her little town permanently.

Centuries later, an idol of Lord Krishna was moved to Rajasthan from Uttar Pradesh for safekeeping by a group of priests. They were transporting the idol on a bullock cart. When the bullock cart reached a particular spot in Mewar, one of its wheels slid into the mud and refused to budge.

The priests said that it was a miracle and it seemed like the god wanted to stay on in that spot. Devotees believe this to be the spot where the divine boy had played with the little princess. The king of Mewar proceeded to build a temple, which was designed like a haveli, just like the one the little princess stayed in when Shrinath would visit her as a boy.

Even today, the Janmashtami celebrations at the Shrinathji Temple in Nathdwara draws a lot of devotees, as it is renowned for Krishna's playful antics and miracles.

Different Krishna temples depict different stages in the god's life. Dwarka is known for Krishna as a king; Kurukshetra, as a warrior; Guruvayur, Govardhan and Nathdwara, as a divine boy; Braj as a lover, and so on.

Vitthal's Footstool

Vitthal Temple, Pandharpur, Maharashtra

Pandharpur, a city in Maharashtra, is famous for its 13th-century Vitthal Temple. Lord Vitthal bears the forms of both Krishna and Vishnu, and, in the main shrine, he is accompanied by an idol of Rakhumai (Rukmini, Krishna's consort).

The idol of Vitthal in the temple is that of a handsome man–boy, standing with his arms akimbo. He has a peaceful look on his face, with a conical cap serving as his crown, wearing *makara kundala* or fish-shaped earrings, garlands of tulsi leaves and a sparkling gem necklace. But the most unusual aspect about this idol is that Vitthal stands on a brick! In fact, some people say the name Vitthal itself means 'one who stands on a brick'.

According to one of the legends in this town, there once lived a man named Pundalik, who was a great devotee of Vitthal. One day, the divine cowherd, Krishna, came over to meet Pundalik at his home, on the banks of the River Bhima. It was mealtime, and Pundalik was busy serving his elderly parents. As his duty to his parents came first, even before his devotion to the lord, Pundalik asked Krishna to wait by the door until he finished serving his parents. He tossed a brick from inside his house to the front steps, and asked the lord to stand on it and wait for a bit.

After he had done his duty, Pundalik hurried to the front door and asked the lord for forgiveness for making him wait. Krishna was pleased by his devotee's sense of duty and told Pundalik that he could ask for any boon he wanted. Pundalik said he would like Vitthal to stay on Earth forever.

Obliging him, Lord Vitthal stayed put at the spot on the brick, around which the temple now stands by the banks of the river.

The Cursed Creator

Brahma Temple, Pushkar, Rajasthan

In Hindu mythology, the three most important gods of the cosmos are Brahma, the creator of the universe, Shiva, the destroyer of evil and Vishnu, the protector of the innocent.

After creating the universe, Brahma set out to perform a yagna to bring peace upon his creation. He dropped a lotus from his hand onto Earth, which sprung into a lake called Pushkar (meaning 'flower from the hand'). Even today, the Pushkar Lake is said to be the most special among all the pilgrimages in India.

As Brahma got ready for his rituals, he was asked to sit down for the fire yagna with his wife, Savitri. But the mischief-maker Narada went to her and gave her the wrong time for when she was required to attend the ritual.

Meanwhile, at Pushkar, when there was no sign of Savitri, Brahma quickly married a girl, Gayatri, that Indra, the god of the heavens, had brought along with him, just so the yagna could be conducted at the auspicious hour.

Savitri finally arrived and, of course, flew into a rage when she saw what Brahma had done. She cursed him, saying that he would not be worshipped in temples like other gods. This is why there are such few temples for Brahma. Pushkar is considered the holiest of those few temples where he's prayed to.

A little further away from the Brahma Temple in Pushkar, there is a temple for Savitri, on the nearby Ratnagiri Hill.

Krishna's Playground

Krishna Janmasthan Temple, Brajbhoomi, Uttar Pradesh

Thousands of Krishna temples, big and small, stand in the twin cities of Mathura and Vrindavan, on the banks of River Yamuna, in Uttar Pradesh. This region is known as Brajbhoomi, and because this is where Krishna is believed to have spent his childhood days, it is also called Krishna Janmabhoomi.

The Krishna Janmasthan Temple is said to be in the spot where the prison complex that held his parents was located.

The evil king Kamsa was warned that the eighth child born of his sister Devaki would kill him, ending the evil he had unleashed on his poor, innocent subjects. He, therefore, imprisoned Devaki and her husband, Vasudeva, and proceeded to murder every child they had.

On the night the eighth child was born, there was a terrible storm, and all sorts of miracles happened. The chains that bound Vasudeva fell off and the prison gates opened miraculously, as the guards fell into a swoon. Vasudeva picked up the divine infant and carried him in a basket over his head to the nearby village of Nandagaon, across the Yamuna, where his friend Nanda and his wife, Yashoda, lived. The couple brought up the divine child as their own.

There are many small shrines in the Krishna Janmasthan temple that depict the story of the birth of Krishna. Others show the pranks he played as a child. The abundance of sweet shops nearby, selling butter and milk sweets, is a nod to Krishna's fondness for butter. And Krishna's dance with Radha and the *gopis*, his childhood playmates, is celebrated here at the time of Holi.

Epic Twins

Ram Tirath Temple, Amritsar, Punjab

It is said that after Rama abandoned Sita after his war with Ravana, she found herself in the hermitage of Valmiki. There, she gave birth to her twins, Lava and Kusha. Valmiki helped Sita bring up her sons and made sure they grew up to be well-educated young men.

A temple for Rama was built at this spot, and a sacred tank nearby is believed to have been built by Hanuman, who came to enquire about his beloved Sita Ma's well-being. People say that he swiped his tail with such force that a *baoli*, or tank, with sweet spring water welled up at the spot.

Shakti's Cave Temple

Mata Vaishno Devi Temple, Jammu

Legend has it that Shakti once took the form of a girl and went up the tall mountains of Trikurta in Jammu to meditate. The girl's name was Vaishnavi, the worshipper of Vishnu.

Meanwhile, a local devotee named Sridhar had a dream in which a goddess asked him to organize a feast in her name. Sridhar was a poor man, and he was worried about feeding the many people arriving at his house for the feast. But, miraculously, there was no dearth! Food continued to be cooked and passed around and eaten in his tiny hut. After the feast was over, Sridhar noticed Vaishnavi emerging from the hut and had a feeling that she had something to do with the miracle.

A wicked yogi called Bhaironath also noticed the young girl at the feast, whose face shone with a divine aura. He followed her up the mountains, and found that she carried bows and arrows and was at ease in the company of wild animals.

Annoyed at Bhaironath's constant observation of her, Vaishnavi shed her avatar, took the form of a warrior goddess and killed him in battle. After the battle, she turned into a rock face and continued to meditate.

The sacred shrine of Mata Vaishno Devi is basically made of three stone heads, symbols of Kali, the destroyer of evil, Lakshmi, the bestower of prosperity, and Saraswati, the giver of wisdom.

Eons later, the Pandava princes were said to have visited the rock shrine and the Mahabharata pays homage to the goddess, with Arjuna praising Mata Vaishno Devi as *Jambookkatak chitya shunityam sannihitalaye* or 'she who dwells in the mountain slope of Jamboo', a word that sounds similar to the Jammu we all know today.

HEAVENLY FEASTS

How often have you eaten food that tastes absolutely delicious and called it 'divine'? Food plays a huge role in the happiness and well-being of human beings. So, it is not surprising that most early human communities and civilizations offered food to their gods as a sacred ritual.

In the ancient world, hunters and farmers offered animals as sacrifice. Even today, among several religions, the first harvest of rice, fruits, vegetables, cereals and nuts are all offered to the gods before devotees eat. Essentially, it is the best of a community's food that is given to the gods as a way of saying thanks. That food is then considered blessed.

Food is an important element in the tales of several ancient civilizations. The ancient Greeks talked about ambrosia, which was considered 'the nectar of the gods' and was served at heavenly feasts. In Greek mythology, there was a nymph named Ambrosia who was turned into a grapevine, and the drink made from the fruits of this vine made the gods immortal. They even had a god of wine called Dionysus.

In the great civilization of ancient Rome, Bacchus, the god of wine and agricultural produce, was one of the most important gods. And priests in Egyptian temples offered meat, vegetables and fruits to their deities. The Egyptians also offered food to their household gods.

Jewish culinary rituals give much importance to bread, wine and olive oil. Various dishes are prepared using these ingredients for special religious occasions and rituals. The Hebrew Bible talks of a special meat prepared as burnt offering (sacrificial food that was cooked and burnt and placed at the altar) at the Temple of Solomon and Hezekiah's Temple in Israel.

At Jinkwansa, a 12th-century Buddhist temple in South Korea, Buddhist nuns prepare a special temple feast, which includes fermented foods, without using any processed ingredients, meat or animal by-products like dairy. The preparation of the food follows the Buddhist dharma, or rules, of non-violence. Such monastic cuisines are believed to aid in meditation and help increase concentration.

In Japan, soy is called the 'food for Buddha', and temple chefs make simple, nourishing fare without meat or dairy in the country's many temples. Called *shojin ryori,* this is the food of Buddhist monks in the temples.

The temple that holds the record for feeding the largest number of people every day is in India. Amritsar's Golden Temple feeds tens of thousands of people every single day. Food is prepared in the *langar*, or community kitchen, of the gurdwara. Cooked by devotees, it is served to all the visitors for free.

Does God eat the food offered by humans in temples? Well, believers say that prasad is the food 'graced by the breath of god'. It really is a symbolic offering, as the food placed before the deity at the temple or shrine is then taken away and eaten by devotees.

It is possible that some of the best food in India has been made in temple kitchens! Some temples are famous for their prasad or *naivedyam*.

Seasonal produce, local spices like pepper, rice, dal, country vegetables and sweets made of milk, curds, *khoya* and jaggery (palm sugar; white sugar was a late

While prasad refers to the sweets, fruits or food offered to the temple deity and distributed to devotees, *naivedyam* is the ritual act of placing food in the shrine before the deity and offering prayers.

discovery) all come together to make Indian temple cuisine taste heavenly.

To know more about the wide variety of temple cuisine and sacred offerings to various gods and goddesses, read on. And do remember to ask about the special food-related story next time you visit a temple and taste its prasad.

The Goddess of Food

Steamed Rice – Annapurna Temple, Varanasi, Uttar Pradesh

One day, the ascetic Shiva told Parvati that the world and everything living in it was all maya (an illusion). 'What's the point of enjoying the material aspects of living when life is temporary?' he wondered aloud.

To prove that life was indeed worth living and nature's bounty was extraordinary, Parvati decided to play a trick on him.

She waved her hand and, in a blink of the eye, all material things vanished off the face of the Earth! Nature and its products, especially life-giving food and nourishment for the body and soul, all disappeared. The Earth soon became parched; nothing grew on it to provide food, and humans suffered from hunger and disease.

Upon seeing this, Shiva immediately understood that life on Earth was truly special. He requested Parvati to undo her spell.

'Oh, golden devi, you're the goddess of nourishment; feed the hungry and come down to Earth,' he implored.

A happy Parvati is said to have appeared in the holy city of Varanasi as Mata Annapurna, the goddess of food. In the Annapurna temple, the deity is often clad in a rich gold casing, and can be found seated holding a golden pot of steamed rice and a golden ladle.

It is believed that Annapurna served Shiva first to make him understand the concept of *anna*, or food, as a metaphor for prosperity and fulfilment.

Blessed Bhog

Mahaprasad – Jagannath Temple, Puri, Odisha

The Jagannath Temple in Puri is special for many reasons, but what truly sets it apart from other temples is the mammoth operation undertaken by its kitchen.

Called *mahaprasad,* the meal here is made of a whopping 56 items, and is cooked by a small army called *mahasupakars.* It is said these chefs don't cook in their own homes, but *only* make food for Lord Jagannath in the temple.

Temples in Odisha are known to run enormous kitchen operations. Seasonal produce, native rice varieties and vegetables such as yam, brinjal and red pumpkin are cooked to perfection and offered as *bhog* at five different times of the day, making sure that the gods are well fed! Unlike prasad, which is a small food offering, the *bhog* is a complete meal.

Chhappan Bhog for Krishna

When Indra unleashed fearsome storms on the villagers of Mathura and flooded their homes, Krishna lifted Mount Govardhan like an umbrella to protect them. After the floods, the villagers showed their appreciation to Krishna by offering him a gigantic meal of 56 items, or *chhappan bhog.* Fruits, sweets (especially *makhan mishri*), dry fruits, nuts, rice and salty snacks are all part of the sacred meal offered in temples to mark this legend.

The *mahaprasad* is called *Anna Brahma*, or the supreme among sacred foods. Cooked in earthenware, it includes cooked rice and lentils with vegetables, a serving of curried vegetables and sweet milk cakes.

Bhog in Eastern India

In West Bengal, Assam and other northeastern states, prasad includes platters of cut fruits like bananas, apples, guavas, pomegranates and raisins and cashewnuts. The *bhog* is a thali of piping hot *kichuri* (cooked rice and dal) and fried vegetables like potatoes or brinjal, papad and kheer.

Ganesha's Big Burp

Modak – Siddhi Vinayak Temple, Mumbai, Maharashtra

Once, Shiva, Parvati and Ganesha visited the hermitage of Sage Atri and his wife, Anasuya. After exchanging pleasantries, they sat down to lunch. That's when trouble started, for the tubby Ganesha complained that he was still hungry even as Anasuya piled their plates high with food.

Little did they know that Ganesha was actually testing Anasuya's patience. Not to be outdone, Anasuya finally brought out a platter of steamed *modaks* from the kitchen.

'What are these?' Ganesha asked.

'Try one,' invited Anasuya.

Ganesha popped one into his mouth and it immediately melted into sweet bliss.

It was a sweet rice-flour dumpling, filled with grated coconut, flavoured with saffron and cardamom, and tossed in a syrup made of jaggery. Unable to stop himself, Ganesha devoured the plate, gobbling up 21 delicious *modak*s in one go, and produced an enormous burp of satisfaction!

The Siddhi Vinayak Temple in Mumbai hosts a grand Ganesh Chaturthi festival in India every autumn. The special temple prasad is 21 steamed *modak*s (or as they say in Marathi, *ukadiche*) offered to the deity amidst loud cries of 'Ganapati Bappa Morya!' or 'Bless us, O big brother Ganapati!'

Saltless Love

Curd Rice – Uppiliappan Temple, Kumbakonam, Tamil Nadu

Most of us don't like food that doesn't have enough salt. But not Vishnu. For him, food tastes of love, not salt, especially if it is prepared by his beloved Lakshmi.

Once, Sage Markandeya prayed fervently to be blessed with the opportunity to witness the divine wedding of

Vishnu and Lakshmi. He performed a severe penance and was soon blessed with a baby girl. He named her Lakshmi and she grew up to be a beautiful maiden.

Vishnu decided to tease the sage. He arrived at Markandeya's doorstep disguised as an old man, and was welcomed inside by the sage and his daughter. The old man, taken in by Lakshmi's beauty, declared that he would like to marry her. Markandeya was shocked, and could not bring himself to say he wanted only Vishnu to marry his Lakshmi.

Vishnu's Prasad

Temples for Vishnu and his avatars in south India have a variety of prasad as offerings.

Sakkarapongal, or sweet rice, at the Parthasarathy Temple, Chennai

Sambara Dosai at the Ranganathaswamy Temple, Srirangam

Kanchipuram Idli at the Varadharaja Perumal Temple, Kanchipuram

Dosai at the Azhagar Kovil, Madurai

Puliodharai, or tamarind rice, at the Cheluvanarayana Swamy Temple, Melukote

Unniappam, a snack made of jaggery, coconut and bananas, at the Padmanabhaswamy Temple, Thiruvananthapuram

Curd rice at the Jagannatha Perumal Temple, Thirumalai

He drummed up an excuse and said, 'Sir, my daughter is too young and playful! She forgets to add salt in the food whilst cooking.'

The old man promptly replied, 'I'm in love and would happily eat saltless food all my wedded life if I were given Lakshmi's hand in marriage.'

The old man then transformed into Vishnu, leaving the sage speechless. Markandeya was overjoyed to learn that his daughter was none other the goddess Lakshmi herself. He thanked them both for coming to Earth to allow him to witness their wondrous wedding.

A temple stands in the town where Markandeya lived and where the divine wedding took place. The Vishnu deity in the temple is the 'saltless' lord, or Uppiliappan in Tamil. The temple prasad is curd rice and vada cooked without salt. All food offered to the deity is made without salt here!

Record-breaking Prasad

Pongal – Attukal Bhagavathy Temple, Thiruvananthapuram, Kerala

The annual spring food festival of Pongala Mahotsavam held in the Attukal Bhagavathy Amman Temple in Kerala has created a world record for the sheer number of people who attend it!

Lakhs and lakhs of women congregate at the annual Pongal (which literally translates to 'boil over' in Tamil) festival, stooping over to stir brass or earthen pots on stoves made of firewood or bricks on the ground, to cook their sacred offering of pongal, a dish made of rice cooked in milk and jaggery syrup, mashed bananas, grated coconut and cardamom.

The temple deity, Attukal Bhagavathy Amman, is a fierce goddess, and is worshipped by women. Legend has it that the Tamil epic heroine Kannagi, after burning down Madurai in anger because the Pandya king had wrongly killed her husband, reached this spot to pray and let her rage cool. The women of the village, having heard of the piety of Kannagi, gathered to welcome her and cooked sweet pongal in her honour.

This scene is played out each year, with the temple's surroundings witnessing the mass cooking of pongal.

Food for the Mind

The Mahadeva Temple in Thrissur, in Kerala, has an unusual prasad. The authorities of the temple believe food for the mind is more important than food for the body, so students and children are given textbooks, writing and study material as prasad!

Eating the Humble Puttu

Puttu – Puttu Chokkanathar Temple, Madurai, Tamil Nadu

Thousands of years ago, Madurai was beset by rains and floods. The king of Madurai decided to build a huge bund across the

River Vaigai to stop the waters from entering the city. To speed up the work, the king ordered every household to send one member to join the work and help in the construction.

Vanthiammai was an old and poor woman, who lived alone. She was an ardent devotee of Chokkanathar (another name for Shiva). She earned a living by making *puttu*, a dish of steamed rice and coconut, and selling it on a street near the temple.

Obeying the king's orders, she hobbled over to the construction site and began carrying sand. It was back-breaking work and soon, Vanthiammai collapsed.

She called out, 'Will any man trade this hard labour with me? I will serve him my tasty *puttu* for free.'

She felt a tap on her shoulder. A handsome and able-bodied young man stood behind her. 'I'll do it,' he said cheerfully. 'But, Amma, I first need the *puttu*. I'm starving.'

Vanthiammai gladly served him saying, 'If only I had a son like you!'

The young man laughed and after eating the *puttu* said, 'Uff, I'm too full to work,' and promptly went to take a nap under a tree on the site.

The king, who was on his rounds to supervise the work, saw the young man snoring and brought his whip down on his back to wake him up.

'Ouch, ow, *aiyo*,' cried out every man on the site, for they all felt the whiplash that had landed on the young man. Why, even the Pandya king shuddered as he felt a sharp, invisible lash on *his* back!

It was a miracle! Chokka, or Shiva, had disguised himself as a young man to help the poor woman who served him the humble steamed *puttu* every day.

The king realized his folly instantly and only allowed able-bodied people to work on the site.

The temple for Shiva in this town is called Puttu Chokkanathar Temple and the annual *puttu* festival, held to mark this temple legend, is attended by hundreds of devotees.

A Treat for Little Girls

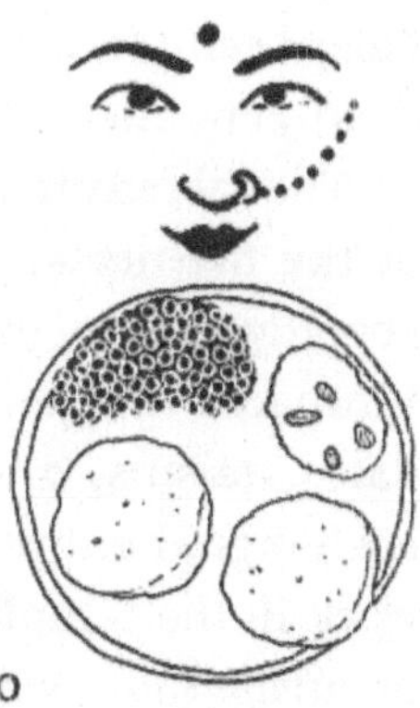

Poori, Chana and Halwa – Vaishno Devi Temple, Jammu

Once Vaishnavi had vanquished the evil Bhaironath, she walked down, battle weary, to a village nearby. The people there were said to have fed her a simple meal of *poori, chana* and *halwa* to help her regain her energy and overcome her fatigue.

While the Mata Vaishno Devi Temple offers dry prasad of sugar balls, *makhana* (puffed lotus seeds) and coconut pieces in tiny plastic packets, devotees often distribute this *poori–chana–halwa* combo to the *kanjak*, the little girls believed to be forms of Goddess Vaishnavi.

The Magical Jam

Panchamritham – Dhandayudhapani Temple, Palani, Tamil Nadu

In ancient Tamil Nadu, the Siddars were a wandering group of hermits, who possessed a deep knowledge of medicine, alchemy and magic. Bhogar was a famous

Siddar who was working on a medicine that could fight the vilest of diseases.

Bhogar's search for healing herbs and plants brought him to the Palani Forest, known for its fruit orchards. He worked with the mysterious herbs and chemicals here, and sculpted the idol of Dhandayudhapani Murugan in the Palani temple using an elixir called *navapashanam* (nine deadly chemicals known to fight diseases).

The sacred offering in this temple is the *panchamritham*, or the five-nectar jam. In the temple kitchen, the jam is actually made of more than five ingredients – bananas from Virupachi village in the Palani hills, jaggery, sugar candy, dates, raisins, ghee and cardamom. The proportion of each ingredient remains a secret known only to those who work in the temple kitchen, and the Palani Murugan idol of *navapashanam* is washed using this sweet jam. It is then offered as a potent prasad to devotees.

The King's Takeaway

Paan – Ram Raja Temple, Orchha, Madhya Pradesh

In the 15th-century kingdom of Orchha, Raja Madhukar Shahjudev's queen, Rani Ganeshkunwari, was an ardent devotee of Lord Rama. Once she went on a pilgrimage to Ayodhya and was so overwhelmed by the darshan of Lord Rama in the temple that she brought back an idol to grace her kingdom.

She set the idol in the queen's quarters in the palace, and sent out a royal order that a grand temple should be built for the god in the kingdom. However, when the time came, the idol of Rama placed in the palace simply could not be moved to the new temple. The royal family, ministers and guards all tried to move the idol, but it wouldn't budge.

That night, Rama appeared in the queen's dream, and told her that he would preside in the palace as the king that he rightfully was. The next day, the king and queen vacated the palace, turning their home into the Ram Raja Temple.

In the shrine that resembles a throne, the deities of Rama, Sita, Lakshmana and Hanuman sit in their royal finery. A daily gun salute marks obeisance to the regal god, as is custom in the royal palace.

Traditionally auspicious occasions are marked by giving guests a thanksgiving betel leaf, or *paan*, as they

Food Garlands for Hanuman

Once Hanuman and Rahu, the serpent god, raced each other to touch the sun. As the son of Vayu the wind god, Hanuman won the race easily. Rahu's favourite cereal is black gram (*urad* dal in Hindi). He said that devotees would henceforth garland Hanuman with food made of *urad* dal. The garland must, however, resemble Rahu's serpentine form to remind the world of their race. Hence, in south Indian temples, Hanuman is offered a vada *mala*, a garland of vadas made of *urad* dal and peppercorns; and garlands of *jalebis*, made of *urad* dal dunked in sugar syrup, adorn Hanuman in some north Indian temples.

leave. In the Ram Raja Temple, besides milk sweets, the prasad is the flavoured *paan* served in royal households.

Purple Prasad

Chak Hao Kheer – Sri Govindajee Temple, Imphal, Manipur

Krishna is known for his boundless love for butter, cream, curd and milk. Temples across India make regional sweet delicacies and offer them to Krishna. One such example of a special food created for the god can be found in Manipur.

Krishna's Sweet Tooth

Temples across India offer special milk-based sweets for Lord Krishna.

Peda – Sri Krishna Janmashtan Temple, Mathura
Pal payasam – Guruvayurappan Temple, Guruvayur
Makhan misri – Bankey Bihari Temple, Vrindavan
Kheer – Radha Raman Temple, Vrindavan
Poha – Dwarkadish Temple, Bet Dwarka
Mathadi – Shrinathji Temple, Rajasthan

Now, the rice we eat at home is usually white in colour. In Manipur, in northeast India, a nutty-flavoured black rice is grown, and it actually looks dark purple when cooked.

At the Sri Govindajee Temple in Imphal, the 19th-century king Maharaja Nara Singh began the ritual of offering *chak hao kheer* as prasad. This is a pudding made of black rice, cooked in milk and sweetened with jaggery or sugar, and flavoured with cardamom and nuts. The temple priests are said to slow cook the pudding and the result is a decadent purple kheer that is both delicious and nutritious!

Blessed Biryani

Biryani – Muniyandisamy Temple, Madurai, Tamil Nadu

The fearsome-looking towering figure of a man with a flourishing moustache at the entrance of many villages in Tamil Nadu is Muniyandisamy or Munieswaran. He is a folk deity often found seated, with protruding eyes, holding aloft a long blade. Temples dedicated to him are open shrines, usually down the road that leads to a village, with huge Muni idols painted in bright colours.

Munis are forms of *bhoota ganas*, or members of Shiva's army. They are half-human, half-otherworldly.

They are capable of magic and are protective deities – they guard villages. Locals mark their festivals by praying to the guardian *muni* and offering him produce, including vegetables, fruits and animals for sacrifice.

Every January, during the harvest festival, the people of the village Vadakkampatti near Madurai offer their famous biryani as prasad to the guardian deity of the Muniyandisamy Temple.

The biryani is made of thousands of kilos of rice, sacrificial chickens and goats and harvested vegetables. Many villagers take on the role of cooks to stir the aromatic rice preparation in huge cauldrons on firewood stoves throughout the night. The biryani is served as breakfast to the villagers after the early morning prayer rituals to their guardian deity.

The Divine *Dosa*

Dosa – Sri Krishna Temple, Udupi, Karnataka

The Udupi Sri Krishna Temple is a sacred destination for thousands of devotees, and the temple is managed by a group of monks ordained by Saint Madhavacharya in the 13th century. The monastic order is called Udupi Mutt.

The Udupi Mutt is famous all over the country for its satvik food (meals that have a calming influence on the body and mind), using local vegetables and lentils. The Udupi temple kitchen is famous for its long list of vegetable curries made of seasonal and country gourds like pumpkins and spuds like sweet potatos and yams, chutneys, sauteed vegetable mixes and bath or rice-based food preparations like bisibele bath. The temple's global export, if one can call it that , is the masala dosa which is world famous today. The original version in the Udupi temple kitchen had the dosa served with a dollop of white butter and a potato mash without onions or garlic.

But such was the taste of this meal that melted in your mouth that Udupi cooks travelled all over the country and began popularizing their cuisine by setting up Udupi eateries. They gave the traditional offering a twist by adding onions to the potatoes, tempered it with curry leaves and chillies, and slipped the mixture into the *dosa*.

Now, who said temple food wasn't world famous?

Laddoo for the Lord

The Tirupati Balaji Temple is famous for its prasad called Srivari laddoo. No one leaves the temple without one of these laddoos. Some 300 years ago, an inventive temple official got the temple cooks to create this offering. Made of *besan*, sugar, ghee, cardamom, nuts and raisins, it tastes heavenly. The large *potu*, or temple kitchen, produces over one lakh laddoos daily that are distributed as prasad to devotees after *naivedyam*.

A Celestial Chappati

Chappati – Ranganathaswamy Temple, Srirangam, Tamil Nadu

In an islet surrounded by the River Cauvery and its tributary Kollidam, stands the Ranganathaswamy Temple

in Srirangam. It is considered the holiest temple in south India by devotees of Lord Vishnu.

In the 14th century, the Sultan of Delhi, Alauddin Khilji, sent his troops to attack the Ranganathaswamy Temple, famed for its wealth and its enormous stores of gold and gems. The temple priests hurriedly hid the main deity and placed the processional idol of Ranganatha in front of the invading army. The soldiers took the idol back to Delhi to show their sultan their loot.

Unbeknownst to everyone else in the court, the sultan's daughter's heart stirred when her eyes fell upon the handsome idol of Lord Ranganatha displayed in the Delhi durbar.

Meanwhile, the troubled people of Srirangam sent a group of temple priests to meet with the sultan to persuade him to return the sacred idol to the temple. The sultan relented, and the priests left for Srirangam, carrying the idol of Ranganatha with them.

Following the priests quietly from the palace was the sultan's daughter, who had fallen in love with the idol and could not be parted from it.

Ranganathaswamy Temple is famous for its variety of temple cuisine, of which the sambara dosai, flavoured with ginger and peppercorns, is most popular. But what's unique is the priest's daily offering of chappatis in honour of a female deity simply called Thuluka Nachiyar or Bibi Nachiyar (the Muslim female saint). Bibi Nachiyar is believed to be the Khilji princess who worshipped Ranganatha.

The prasad of the north Indian chappati offered in a south Indian temple shows us how sacred food links regions, cultures and cuisines.

The Divine Doctor

Mukkudi – Dhanwanthari Temple, Thrissur, Kerala

In the village of Nelluvai, straddled between emerald-green paddy fields and a murmuring brook, there is a temple for Lord Dhanwanthari, the divine doctor.

Once, the asuras and the devas churned the ocean of milk for the nectar of immortality. They used Mount Mandara as a fulcrum and twisted the divine serpent Vasuki as a rope. The devas held on to the tail of the super serpent and the asuras held his mouth. The churning threw up many things. All sorts of celestial beings, animals, plants, gems and other magical things began to emerge from the ocean. Dhanwanthari was one of those divine beings. Believed to be a form of Maha Vishnu, he came out of the ocean carrying a pot of elixir. He is is considered to be an expert in Ayurveda, the ancient Indian science of healing and medicine using natural herbs.

Dhanwanthari is hailed as the doctor of the devas and is seen in the form of Vishnu with four arms. One arm holds a conch, another a discus, the sacred weapons of Vishnu. The third hand holds nectar and the fourth, a leech. (In olden times, leeches were placed on people with diseases as it was believed that the moment the worms sucked their blood, the infections would be cured.)

At the Dhanwanthari Temple in Thrissur, the daily offering is called Mukkudi, a sacred tonic. It is a medicinal formula with curd, turmeric, peppercorn powder, salt and secret herbs, offered to the deity during the morning puja. This is then sanctified and given to devotees as blessed medicine.

The Mystery of the Cold Drink

Panakala Narasimha Swamy Temple, Mangalagiri, Andhra Pradesh

When we are angry we are told to drink some cold water, aren't we?

Lord Narasimha too needed a drink after he mauled Hiranyakashipu to death, roaring in anger. His throat was parched!

'Pankala' in Telugu is the name of a drink made of water sweetened with jaggery syrup and flavoured with cardamom. It is a cold drink offered to cool the anger of Lord Narasimha Swamy at the temple in Mangalagiri as sacred prasad. And devotees believe that the leonine idol of Narasimha Swamy drinks it, as if by magic!

Inside the shrine, the idol of Narasimha Swamy is encased in gold. But the deity's mouth is not covered in gold. It is left open, and priests pour glasses of panakala into it. They believe that once Narasimha Swamy has had his fill, the excess drink mysteriously seeps out of his mouth! Every day pilgrims are offered glasses of this panakala as a holy drink after the deity has 'taken a sip'.

GREEN DEITIES

One of the earliest forms of worship among humans was the worship of nature – animals, water, the wind, rain and even the sun were all seen as divine symbols. But plants and jungles have always held a special place in human life, across continents and civilizations. Forests were seen as places ruled by mysterious laws beyond human comprehension.

Many European folktales and fairy tales are set in forests, replete with magical trees and plants. For example, the Mediterranean olive tree was very important in the Greek civilization, and was considered sacred by them. The term 'to offer an olive branch' means to bring in peace by renewing friendly ties with someone or something.

The ancient Romans had sacred groves where cults, groups of people who practised unusual forms of magic, met. Greek and Roman gods and emperors wore flowers as decorative headpieces. Laurel, oak, myrtle and grass crowns were worn as marks of honour and victory. Flora was worshipped as the Roman goddess of flowers and vegetation.

Druids, magicians whose rituals involved plants and forests, were an important part of the Gaul and Celtic tribes of Europe. The Celtics also worshipped Nemetona, the goddess of sacred groves. Native religion followers in Estonia, in northern Europe, worship thousands of forests as sacred groves even now.

In Japan, the Shinto people built shrines in sacred groves of cryptomeria trees. In southern China, near Yunnan, the Sani people worship Mizhi, a local deity of sacred forests. In Africa, many jungles are still deemed sacred, especially in Ghana.

In India, there are over 15,000 well-documented sacred groves. They are divided into *tapovan* (forests for sages and ascetics to offer penance), *mahavan* (jungle sanctuaries), and *shrivan* (sacred groves).

Indian temples have a close relationship with forests. Many temples have their own trees, called *sthalavriksha*. Most gods in temples are associated with particular plants, trees, flowers, fruits, seeds and other forms of flora.

Stories about *sthalavriksha*s show that safeguarding the environment was as important for the ancients as it is for us today. The following stories tell us that caring for various species of flora and fauna and protecting nature and its bounty are sacred duties.

Goddess of the Forests

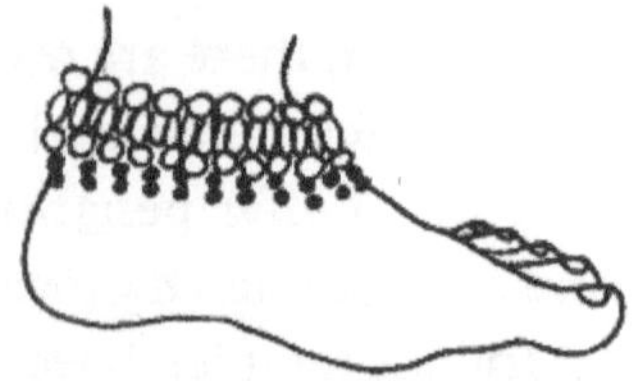

Aranya Devi Temple, Arrah, Bihar

Meet Aranyani, the goddess of forests. She is worthy of worship for being the guardian deity of sacred sanctuaries, woodlands and jungles.

Forests are considered to be the home of female energy, or Goddess Shakti. They are believed to function under the protective control of female spirits, who can be both fierce and benign. In Bengali, the guardian spirit of the forest is called *bonobibi* and in Kannada, she is called Vana Durga.

Aranya means 'forest' in Sanskrit. While most of us fear wild places, Goddess Aranyani is fearless, dwelling in the jungle amongst the fiercest of beasts and the most dangerous of terrains.

And don't for a single moment think she prances about in grass skirts with green creepers twirled around her for jewellery! For Aranyani is most mysterious, as she is known to love to dance but can never be seen by the human eye. Villagers around her forests insist that they have heard her anklets tinkling as she goes traipsing about, leaves rustling on the forest floor after her footsteps.

The Aranya Devi Temple stands in a little town called Arrah in Bihar. Arrah comes from the Hindi word for saw, the serrated blade used to cut wood and mighty tree trunks.

This area was once the kingdom of Raja Mordhwaj. The king and queen desperately wanted a child, so they prayed to Goddess Durga, who appeared one night in the king's dream and blessed him. Soon, the queen had a baby boy.

Their joy knew no bounds as they watched the young prince grow. One night, Durga appeared in Raja Mordhwaj's dream again. This time, she had a painful demand. She wanted the king and queen to saw the prince in half and offer his flesh as sacrifice.

Unwavering in their devotion, the king and queen decided to fulfil the demand, and their son too was ready to offer his flesh to the goddess. The next day, the prince was made to stand at the palace altar, and the king and queen placed a saw over his shoulder. At that precise moment, Goddess Durga appeared before them and said that her cruel trick was only to test their faith in her, and she blessed the family with eternal happiness. The spot where the sacrifice was to have taken place was from that moment known as Arrah, or 'the place of the saw'.

The east-facing temple in Arrah has a main shrine that houses not one but two idols of the goddesses Aranya Devi,

Gods and Their Forests

Many gods are associated with different kinds of forests.

Shakti	*Neem*, or margosa woods
Durga	*Imli*, or tamarind forests
Ganesha	*Ikshu vana*, or sugarcane forests
Shiva	*Daruka vana*, or woods of cedar trees
Krishna	*Vrinda vana*, or woods of basil bushes
Hadimba Devi	*Devadaru*, or deodar forests

who are worshipped as sister goddesses and are made of black stone.

A Forest in the Clouds

Lawkyntang, Mawphalang, Meghalaya

Meghalaya, or the abode of the clouds, is one of the most densely forested areas in India. The Khasi tribe of this region believes that in the sacred grove of Lawkyntang lives U Ryngkew U Basa, the goddess of the woods, who offers sanctuary to all living creatures in this lush jungle.

Lawkyntang, or the sacred forest, in Mawphalang is breathtakingly beautiful and is one of the largest sacred groves in India.

Imagine a temple, open to the skies, surrounded by trees, shrubs, ferns, orchids and tall grasses in the sharpest and deepest shade of green, its floor carpeted with moist lichens and algae!

The trees inside this forest look very much like old and wise sages, who sit deep in meditation – their ancient and gnarled trunks and roots covered in white fungus, trailing like silver beards. Their silent presence adds to the mystery of the woods. There are megaliths, or large oblong stones, revered by the people, scattered across the forest, suggesting that objects such as ancient fossils, stone, rock and cave formations, roots and leaves are all held sacred here.

Locals believe that going into the forest to forage for food or gather firewood will anger U Ryngkew, for she is fiercely protective of the forest and is believed to punish those who spoil the pristine beauty of the area.

Blessed Botanicals

Banashankari Temple, Bagalkot, Karnataka

In the Tilakaranya forest, near the heritage town of Badami in Karnataka, stands a temple to the green goddess of vegetables, roots, tubers and fibres. Known as Banashankari (the goddess of forests), she is also worshipped as Shakambari, or the goddess of veggies.

There was a demon called Durgamasura, who terrorized the innocent people of the area. The gods appealed to Shiva, who sent forth Durga as Banashankari from a sacred fire. She challenged the demon to a fight and, after a fierce battle, killed him in the spot where the temple now stands.

The Tilakaranya Forest has a profusion of tropical trees, like coconut, banana, palm, mango and neem. Once, during a drought, when people were starving, the goddess appeared in the form of Shakambari and fed the villagers fruits and vegetables.

Every winter, the temple hosts a Banashankari *jatre*, a cultural occasion. The temple and its surroundings are decorated with flowers and leaves of mango, neem, banana and *bel* trees. On the occasion of Palleda Habba, or the

The Neem Goddess

The neem or margosa tree is considered sacred in India. Herbalists and village doctors consider its oil, leaves and bark medicinal. The neem tree is worshipped as a botanical form of Goddess Shakti to ward off poxes. In the Goddess Mariamman temples of Tamil Nadu, a neem festival is held every year, in which female devotees wear neem skirts and circle and dance around the shrine carrying fire pots.

vegetable festival, the goddess is worshipped with 108 kinds of vegetable dishes!

Guardians of the Groves

Guru Jambheshwar Bhagwan Mandir, Banar, Rajasthan

Now Rajasthan may instantly conjure up images of sandy dunes, thorny trees and thirsty camels, but did you know that in and around the Thar Desert there are actually sacred forests called *oran*? These forested areas are dotted with the evergreen thorny *khejri* trees, desert trees, that are fiercely guarded by the Bishnois, or devotees of Vishnu.

In the 18th century, a king wanted to cut the *khejri* woods to build a city. A Bishnoi woman, Amrita Devi, and her daughters fell upon their beloved *khejri* trees, hugging them tightly and offering their necks to be lopped off in place of the trees when the king's men brought their axes to cut the trees.

Roused by their piety, over 300 Bishnois soon joined the protest and offered their lives instead of the trees to the king's men. The Bishnois are credited with starting the Chipko Movement, or Save the Trees campaign, in India, and the village Khejarli is named after the trees.

Bishnoi men are traditionally clothed in white. Some say the Bishnois don't want to use plants like indigo for frivolous reasons like dying their garments blue!

The Bishnois pray to and follow the teachings of their founding father, Guru Jambheshwar. The guru's preaching is called *shabad vani,* and it includes the sermon of protecting sacred forests, especially woods of *khejri* trees.

The Guru Jambheshwar Bhagwan Mandir in Banar, near Jodhpur, is set in a peaceful grove. The quiet temple, with the *sthalavriksha* of *khejri* trees, has deer and peacocks and draws the Bishnois in the thousands for worship.

Smoking Hot Fruits for Granny

Pazhamudirsolai Murugan Temple, Madurai, Tamil Nadu

It was a blazing hot afternoon in the hills. The sun spared none, roasting man and beast alike.

The old and grey Avvai was a clever poetess and songwriter. She was proud of the fact that she was a wordsmith and that her wit was second to none.

Avvai was travelling along a hilly region one day, filled with herbal forests and orchards, whose fruits perfumed the air with their sweet scent. *Aiyo*! What wouldn't she give to quench her thirst with one of the juicy fruits from this wild orchard?

She halted under a large berry tree with a canopy that provided shelter from the sun. She sat down at its base to stretch her old legs and rest her back against its big bark. Then, she shut her eyes and sighed.

'Granny! Want a fruit?'

Avvai jumped at the sudden voice and looked around.

'Oi! Up here,' said the voice.

She looked up to see a sweet-looking tribal boy swinging on one of the tree's top branches, sucking on a berry.

'Oh yes, please be a dear and drop a handful of berries for me,' she said.

'What kind do you want?'

'What kind is there?' Avvai wondered aloud, finding the question silly.

'Do you want a smoked fruit or a non-smoked one?' he asked.

Avvai was annoyed at his cheekiness, but decided to play along. 'How about a smoked one, then?' she replied. She was rewarded with a shower of berries as the boy gave the branches a good shake. She picked up a few fallen berries off the ground, and cupping them in her palms, puffed and blew the dust off them.

'Smoking hot, aren't they?' said the boy with a chuckle.

Avvai froze. That pun was so witty! This little fella was not silly; he was mocking *her* with his clever word play!

The berries slid out of her hands as Avvai stood up reverentially and looked up.

'Who are you? You're not the boy you're pretending to be,' she said, her pride having been put firmly in place.

'Right you are, Avvai!' laughed the boy as he morphed into his divine form.

It was Muruga, Avvai's favourite god, who had decided to match his wits with hers that afternoon!

Avvai's eyes filled with tears of joy and she hailed Murugan as the lord of the orchards.

The Pazhamudirsolai Murugan Temple, called the temple of the orchards, stands in the hilly forests where Avvai was given 'smoked' fruits by Murugan, and is surrounded by forests, springs, wild monkeys and tribal hamlets.

The Green Goddess

Hariyali Devi Temple, Chamoli, Uttarakhand

The night was awash with an inky blackness. The messenger hurried under the cover of darkness to the evil king Kamsa's chamber, to give him news that his sister, Devaki, had just given birth to her seventh child.

On hearing the news, Kamsa rolled off his bed, grabbed his sword and rushed to the jail where he'd imprisoned Devaki. He wanted to kill all of his sister's children as soon as they were born, as he was cursed to be killed by one of them.

He halted in the prison cell to see his sister sobbing uncontrollably, clutching a beautiful baby girl in her arms. With a roar, Kamsa grabbed the infant but she slipped out of his hands, flew up into the sky, and morphed into a goddess.

'Fool! It is not I, but my brother born after me, who will kill you,' she warned him ominously before disappearing.

No one knew where she had vanished into the night air. But up in the pristine mountains of Uttarakhand, in the village of Chamoli, the villagers knew. She had appeared atop the peak of the nearby mountain and stayed in the spot where the Hariyali Devi Mandir stands today – on Hari's mountain, named after her brother.

The mountain people venerate her as Hariyali Devi, or the bountiful goddess, a form of Durga who protects the area. There are enchanted sacred groves full of pine and oak trees and woody plants like rhododendrons on this mountain. Medicinal herbs are also known to grow here.

Beware, for you will be shooed away if your last meal was laced with the pungent aromas of meat, garlic and onions! Hariyali Devi is known to prefer only the sweet smells of vegetables and fruits in her forest.

Firewood is not gathered from this forest and don't even think of plucking twigs and leaves during your treks for keepsakes. Villagers will warn you with the story of the woman who fell ill after picking firewood from the forest.

Nothing leaves the sacred forest because her devotees believe that Goddess Hariyali Devi will punish them for depleting her forest cover.

A Sacred Wonder in the Woods

Unakotishwara Kal Bhairav Rock Face, Unakoti, Tripura

Once, Shiva was travelling with a huge entourage of gods, *bhoota ganas* and spirits, when they passed through the forests of Jampui Hill on the way to Mount Kailasha.

The area was encircled by the Manu River in north Tripura, and dotted with gurgling waterfalls, rocky boulders and wild vegetation.

It had been a long day, and Shiva and party decided to spend the night at this spot. Shiva told his group of 99,99,999, or *unakoti* (less than a crore), to rest for the night but wake up at the crack of dawn to continue the journey.

Dawn broke, golden lines of sunlight streaking the blue sky, but the *unakoti* were still snoring. An irritated Shiva cursed them to stay there as stones and left in a huff. The sculpted rock faces are now venerated as a Saiva shrine for Unakotishwara Kal Bhairav in the northeast. To mark the sacred spot, the place is called Unakoti after the folktale.

The most extraordinary sight of the huge sculpted faces of Shiva, Durga, Ganesha and other celestial beings on flat rock faces greets visitors in this landscaped forest. Called bas relief, these are sacred open-air rock shrines – washed by the pure rains, cooled by the crisp mountain air and worshipped with the fresh forest greenery.

According to another folktale, there once lived a sculptor called Kallu Kumar, who was a great devotee of Parvati. He wanted to follow Shiva and Parvati to their abode in

Kailasha. Shiva threw him a challenge – to sculpt ten million images of various gods and goddesses overnight if Kallu Kumar wanted to attain *moksha*, or salvation, and join them in Kailasha.

Kallu Kumar worked very hard through the night but alas, when the sun came up, he was short of one crore sculpted rocks. Since he had failed, Shiva returned to Kailasha, leaving behind the rock imprints in Unakoti.

The Tears and Tempers of Shiva

Shiva is called Rudra or the god of wrath as he loses his temper easily. He is offered leaves of the *bel* or *vilva* tree, known for its cooling properties, for worship. *Bel* sherbet is a cooling drink that is made in the summers!

Shiva wears *rudraksha* beads that are said to be the tears that rolled down his cheeks and dropped on Earth and grew into the plants bearing *rudraksha* seeds.

Herbal Plunder

Dunagiri Devi Temple, Almora, Uttarakhand

It was a day of utter disaster on the battlefield. Rama's dearest brother, Lakshmana, had been struck down by a poisoned arrow shot by Ravana's son Indrajit.

The royal physician, Sushena, examined the unconscious Lakshmana and said the only potion to revive him was the *sanjeevni booti*, or the herbal medicine made from the four sacred herbs of *mruta sanjeevni* (life-nurturing herb), *vishalyakarani* (for poisoned arrow wounds), *savarnvakarani* (for glowing skin) and *sandhanakarani* (to revive the skin).

These, Sushena said, were found only on the Dunagiri Hill in the Himalayan mountain range.

'Hurry now, for there's no time to waste,' Sushena appealed to Hanuman, or Vayuputra, who could fly as fast as the wind.

As Hanuman grew in size to touch the heavens, far beyond the clouds, and soar away, Sushena called out to him, 'You can spot them easily as the herbal hills will glow in the dark.'

Alas, the directions did not help, for Hanuman was no botanist. He could not tell the difference from one plant and another. He landed on Dunagiri, or the 'divine mountain', and scratched his head in confusion at the sight of so many aromatic herbs growing around, not knowing which one was a healing herb and which one was poisonous!

The sacred herbal forest was under the protection of Dunagiri Devi. The groves were also a laboratory for Ayurvedic sages, to experiment with herbal remedies, and mix medicinal potions and make curative preserves. The Bhutia tribes of the hills were protective of the herbs that grew in their devi's sacred groves.

Hanuman asked the locals for directions to pluck the herbs for the *sanjeevni booti*. They remained tight-lipped, refusing to help him. Who was this giant simian anyway? A foreigner, obviously, landing in their home, demanding to yank out medicinal herbs from their sacred forests!

Dejected, Hanuman stomped around the village in Almora, and found an old woman sitting on the mountain side. He unburdened his heart and told her why he needed the herbs for the *sanjeevni booti* so desperately. The crone was moved by his tale, so she took him to the forest and showed him the hillock where the herbs grew.

An overjoyed Hanuman didn't wait to find the four herbs that Sushena asked him to bring back. Instead, he hastily picked up the entire herbal hillock and flew away towards Lanka!

The locals were terribly angry with the giant monkey, divine creature or not, for plundering a portion of their sacred forest. They decided that no one from their mountainside would ever worship Hanuman.

So even today, the only temple that crowns the mountain is the shrine of Dunagiri Devi, whose protective gaze keeps a firm eye on the verdant Himalayan forests.

Betel Leaf Garlands for Hanuman

After the war in Lanka was over, when Hanuman came to lead Sita back to Rama, she wanted to show her appreciation for all his help. Not finding much around her in the garden of Ashoka trees where Ravana had imprisoned her, Sita quickly plucked the leaves of a betel creeper nearby and wove it into a garland. She greeted Hanuman with the garland, and this moved him deeply. Since then, betel leaf garlands have been used as special offerings in Hanuman temples.

Narmada's Garden

Narmada Udgam Temple, Amarkantak, Madhya Pradesh

The Amarkantak Valley lies nestled in the wildlife sanctuary near Maikal Hills. It is surrounded by wild fruit orchards, flowering shrubs and herbs, gurgling brooks and ponds watered by the Narmada, Johila and Son rivers. Devotees call it a *theerthraj* ('king of all pilgrimages').

It was in these beautiful natural surroundings that Shiva chose to meditate. His concentration was so intense that beads of sweat collected all over him and gathered into a *kund*, or pool, that swelled and flowed as the River Narmada. Amarkantak is thus worshipped as the fount of the mighty River Narmada.

Legend has it that Goddess Narmada appeared in the dream of a nomad called Rewa Nayak, asking him to clear a site in the jungle and build her a temple by the *kund*.

The Narmada Udgam Temple is a group of shrines, with towers painted with white lime, standing by a pond. They form a striking, austere image, against the emerald-hued forests all around. There are two shrines in this complex for Goddess Narmada. There are shrines for Shiva and also a clutch of lingams near the *kund*.

Locals call the woods near the temple *Ma ki Bagiya*, or the divine mother's garden, where Narmada is known to spend time plucking sweet-smelling flowers, fruits like mangoes tasted by the beaks of parrots, and aromatic herbs.

Sacred Floral Offerings

marigold - Ganesha
datura, oleander - Shiva
parijata, kadamba - Vishnu, Lakshmi
lotus, tuberose - Lakshmi
palash, rose, allamanda - Saraswati
jasmine - Hanuman
hibiscus, *champa*, passiflora - Shakti
nerium oleander - Karthikeya

A Forest for the Divine Demoness

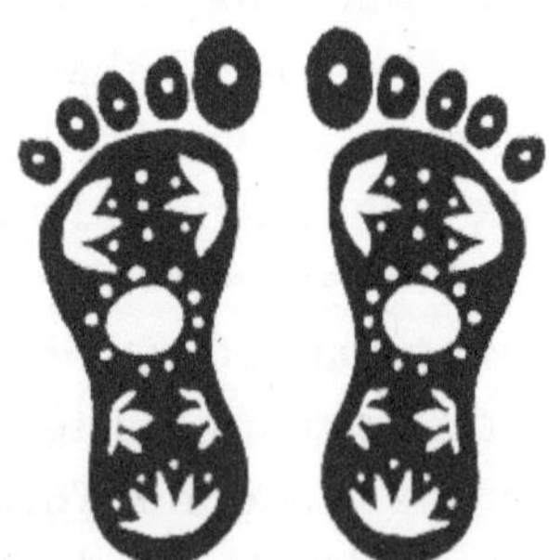

Hidimba Devi Temple, Manali, Himachal Pradesh

The Himalayan state of Himachal Pradesh is called *dev bhoomi*, the land where the gods reside, by devotees. Here, not just gods but even demons and spirits find a home in the hundreds of sacred forests of the state. It's a natural wonderland of caves and mountains, rivers and snow-clad peaks, herbs and sacred plants, and rare birds and animals.

The five Pandava brothers were in exile, choosing to move in secret from one forest to another, in a bid to protect themselves from their evil Kaurava cousins. When they reached the Manali forests, their presence was challenged by the demon Hidimb, who lived there with his sister.

Bhima, the mighty warrior, entered into mortal combat with Hidimb and slayed him. His sister, Hidimba, had vowed that she would marry the person who was as strong as her brother. Bhima and Hidimba got married in the forest and were blessed with a son, Ghatotkacha the demon warrior (who later fought in the Kurukshetra war with his father and uncles).

However, when it was time for Bhima to leave the forest with his brothers, Hidimba chose to stay behind in her home in the forest and meditate.

At the foot of the Himalayas lies a lush cedar sanctuary called Dhungiri Van Vihar. This forest is marked by an unusual Hidimba Devi Temple. The stone structure is crowned by a series of slatted conical towers, or *shikars*, made of wood, with animal skulls strung on the walls, creating a primitive and woodsy picture against the tall trees in the background.

There is no deity in the shrine, but a cave with a rock face bearing the footprints of Hidimba, the patron celestial being of the area. The temple is popular for its Navaratri festivities in autumn, where Hidimba is worshipped as a form of Durga.

The Hunter's Eye for Devotion

Kannappa Temple, Srikalahasti, Andhra Pradesh

On the Srikalahasti Hill in Andhra Pradesh, there was a forest shrine. Every day the priest, Sivakasariar, would climb the hill, clean and bathe the lingam with water from the river Swarnamukhi he carried in a jug. He would pluck the best flowers and string them into garlands for the deity; he would offer fresh uncut fruits and coconuts to Shiva as sacred offerings.

Sivakasariar was very particular about carrying out the purification rituals of worship. The shrine was extremely clean and decorated beautifully. Perfumed sacred ash mixed with rose water was sprinkled on the lingam every day; fragrant flowers were placed at several places in the shrine; and incense sticks and earthen lamps were lit before the deity during prayer time.

One morning he walked up to the shrine as usual, only to recoil in horror. He saw raw flesh from a boar on the offering platter, cactus flowers and weeds strewn around the shrine and water pooling in a puddle on the lingam.

Horrified by the desecration, the furious priest set about cleaning the shrine and offered extra prayers before leaving for the day.

The next morning, a new horror awaited him! The bleeding carcass of a deer lay before the lingam, and thorny plants were again strewn around the deity.

Sivakasariar fell to his knees, sobbed at the defilement and cursed whoever had done this. Unable to bear the sight of his beloved temple and deity in such a mess, he left.

That night, Shiva appeared in Sivakasariar's dream and said, 'Devotion is selfless and innocent. Come early tomorrow morning, during the *Brahma muhurtham*, and see for yourself!'

And so Sivakasariar woke up early at *Brahma muhurtham* (pre-dawn), and went to the forest. He hid behind a bush near the shrine and waited.

At the crack of dawn, a dark figure loomed near the hill. Dusty and grubby, carrying a bleeding animal in one hand, his bow and arrows in the other was Dinna, the hunter of the forest. His face was puffed up, as though he had something in his mouth.

Eshwara! Sivakasariar was shocked to see Dinna lurch forward and spit water from his mouth on the lingam – his hands were obviously full, how else could he carry the water? He tossed the freshly hunted animal before the lord, plucked some weeds and wild flowers from his matted dreadlocks and placed them around the deity.

Great! This is how the crude forester offered worship! Sivakasariar gritted his teeth in anger.

'*Shivappa*!' Dinna called out loudly, sitting down and stretching his legs before the shrine. 'Since I found you alone and unloved in the forest last week, all I think about is taking care of you.

'Do you want to know what happened this morning? This fox was crafty and tried to evade me, but I ran fast and hunted him down. You must be hungry for breakfast, so I came running up the hill. This is good food. You will go hungry with those bananas and coconuts that only monkeys eat! Haw! Haw!' He roared with laughter at his own joke.

Sivakasariar shuddered. This uncouth hunter was coarse down to the last bone in his body. What was this familiar conversation he was having with God, as though he was chatting with a friend? It was not an acceptable expression of devotion. The illiterate fellow obviously does not know Vedic hymns and *shlokas*! thought a livid Sivakasariar.

Suddenly, he heard an anguished wail from Dinna.

'*Appa*, who hurt you?' cried Dinna, as blood suddenly trickled from the right eye of the lingam.

He rubbed at the eye, but the bleeding did not stop. He tried placing herbal leaves from the forest on it, but the bleeding still would not stop. Suddenly, in the midst of his torment, Dinna had a brainwave!

Without any hesitation, he used his arrow and scooped out his own eye and placed it on the lingam. The bleeding stopped immediately! Dinna, his face streaked with blood, danced with joy that his Shivappa's eye had been healed.

Mid-dance he stopped abruptly to see the left eye of the lingam bleeding. Dinna did not stop to think even for a moment. He only had to offer his other good eye to Shiva to stop the bleeding. But if he gouged out his left eye, he would go blind and would not know the correct spot to place his eye on the lingam.

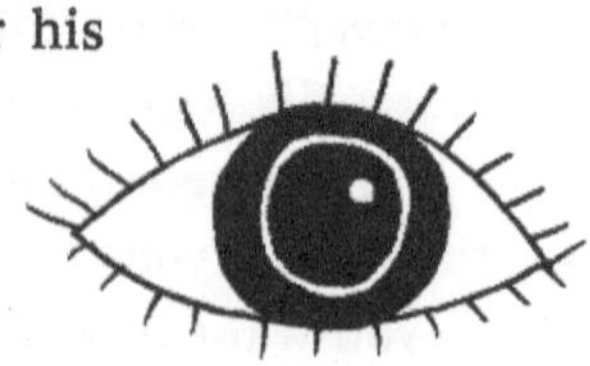

Again, Dinna had a brainwave. He went to the lingam and placed his toe on the bleeding eye, so he would know where to place his eye to halt Shiva's bleeding.

From his hiding place, Sivakasariar was moved by the fierce devotion and love on display before him. Here was a hunter who didn't care if he lost his eyes as long as he could protect his *eshwar*. His devotion was selfless, far beyond the rigid rituals for worship.

Even as Dinna aimed an arrow at his eye, Lord Shiva appeared before him and stopped him. He restored Dinna's eyesight and said that from that point on, the hunter would be known as Kannappa or 'he who offered his eye to the lord'.

Called *girivanam*, or the forest hill shrine, the Kannappa Temple at Srikalahasti is a sacred Shiva *sthala*. It is a reminder that the mark of true devotion is the selfless love of Dinna, the forest hunter.

A Golden Goddess of the Grove

Kanak Durga Temple, Chilkigarh, West Bengal

There once lived a king called Gopinath in Chilkigarh, known for its rich heritage and fertile forests. One night, the goddess Mahamaya, or Devi Chandi, the original form of Shakti, appeared in the king's dream and expressed her wish to have a temple dedicated to her in the forest.

The next morning, two men, Jogendranath and Kamilya, visited the king's court and said they had also had a dream in which Devi Chandi had appeared and ordered them to sculpt and carve a temple in the same spot.

The king ordered the two to get to work immediately, and a temple called Baramahal was built near an ancient banyan tree in these verdant woods.

Soon, miracles began to happen around the temple. When the region was afflicted with drought and the land turned barren, the tribals prayed to Devi Chandi and were rewarded with rains that restored the area's green cover.

Another time, a local priest, who officiated the worship at the temple, worried out aloud that he was afraid to return home each night after prayers as the forest was dark and scary. Devi Chandi appeared in his dream and directed him to go home without any fear as she would protect him, but on the condition that he did not turn around or look back. From then on, the priest walked home in peace through the wild jungle, knowing who was watching his back!

Some 300 years ago, as the temple, weathered by the forest and the elements, crumbled, a king called Kamalkanta shifted the idol of the goddess and placed it in a new temple. The king encased the original stone idol in a glowing cover made of gold, and since then she has been called Kanak Durga, or the golden one.

Chilkigarh is wedged between the River Dulong and dense sacred forests that are home to chattering monkeys and over 400 medicinal herbs. The jungles are also home to several tribes who have lived in the area for

A Floral Tongue

Goddess Kali is always worshipped with a garland of 108 red hibiscus in West Bengal, Odisha and other places in the north and east of India. It is said that the flower's petals resemble the crimson tongue of the goddess and match her fierce temper!

centuries. In this forest, stands the ancient temple of Kanak Durga.

The Kanak Durga Temple follows both tribal and Vedic rituals of worship in deference to the rights of the forest people over their deity and the rituals followed by the kings who built the temple.

A Sacred Sanctuary

Tulsi Shyam Mandir, Gir, Gujarat

Imagine a temple in the middle of a forest full of lions! Fear not, for the Tulsi Shyam Temple in Gir is a famous pilgrimage destination near the sanctuary, and pilgrims are quite safe from wild beasts.

In this forest, there once lived a demon called Tul, who made life for the people of the forest miserable. Tul was very arrogant for he considered himself the most powerful. Krishna (who is also known as Shyam, the dark one) decided to put an end to Tul's atrocities and challenged the demon to a battle. A fierce fight ensued before Krishna emerged the victor and vanquished the demon. An ancient temple was built in celebration of Krishna's victory over evil, and was called the Tulsi Shyam Temple.

The temple deity is believed to be thousands of years old and is a dark stone idol of Krishna. The current temple structure stands in the middle of a forest, on a hillock that can be reached by a steep flight of about a hundred steps. It is also known for the hot springs nearby. They are considered sacred as they are believed to have healing properties.

Krishna's Tulsi

Vishnu and his avatars, like Rama and Krishna, are always worshipped with *tulsi* (holy basil) leaves. The purple-tinted variety is called Krishna *tulsi* as its leaves are as dark as Krishna himself. Tulsi, also called *Vrinda*, is considered a plant form of Goddess Lakshmi, and hence is so loved by Vishnu.

The Sacred Mango Tree

Ekambareshwar Temple, Kanchipuram, Tamil Nadu

The *sthalavriksha* in the Ekambareshwar Temple in Kanchipuram is a mango tree believed to be over thousands of years old! This famous pilgrimage spot has a temple for Shiva in his earthly element, in the company of his wife Parvati as Gowri, the beauteous one, and tells the story of their eternal love.

The story goes that Goddess Parvati came down from Mount Kailash to Kanchipuram, chose a large mango tree, which yielded four different varieties of sweet mangoes, and settled down in its shade to do her penance. She fashioned a lingam out of earth under the tree and began to meditate.

The river Vegavati decided to put Parvati's affection for Shiva to the test. Its waters lashed and flooded

Kanchipuram, and as they pounded against everything, the river also tried to wash away the lingam. Parvati instantly fell upon the lingam and embraced it tightly, protecting it against the angry floods.

Shiva melted at her gesture and rushed to Kanchipuram to join her. He held a grand ceremony (a destination wedding of sorts!) in this temple as Ekambareshwar, or the lord of the mango tree, to wed Parvati as Goddess Gowri.

Gods in the Ghats

Bhimashankar Temple, Sahyadri Hills, Maharashtra

The Western Ghats tower behind the Bhimashankar Wildlife Sanctuary, casting their shadows over the forests and animals. The woods in the sanctuary are famous for their sacred groves.

A trio of demons called Tripurasura harassed the people who lived in the forests there. The gods requested Shiva to help. He took the form of Bhimashankar, or the mighty Shankar, to slay the demons. Once he defeated them, his devotees asked him to stay there and bless the spot. They built a temple in his honour.

Bhimashankar is a form of Shiva worshipped by the Mahadev Koli tribe. It's a *jyotirlinga* temple near the River Bhima and attracts many devotees. The temple overlooks the valleys of the green Sahyadri mountains. These mountains are famous for the various species of plants and trees that grow there, which are protected, as they are considered sacred.

The Magic and Mystery of Forests

Bhagavathy Temple, Thiruvarkadu, Kerala

In Kerala, there are over hundreds of sacred groves called *kavu*. Temple traditions in the state include the practice of occult, tantric and serpent worship. Mostly, they are important places for worshipping the mother goddess, or Bhagavathy Amman.

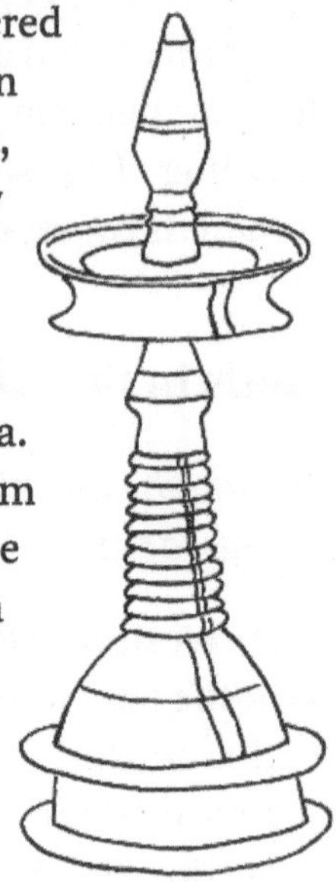

Once, King Madayi was in deep trouble over a demon called Darika. He invoked Shakti, who took the form of Madayi Kavilamma and vanquished the demon. After that, she requested that a shrine be built for her and Shiva.

Shiva's devotee and disciple Parashurama built a shrine for the goddess and Shiva. This temple is considered very powerful by devotees. The presiding deity in the shrine is the Bhagavathy Amman, though the name of the temple town Thiruvarkadu means 'Shiva's forest'. This temple is for one of the fiercest forms of Bhagavathy Amman, or Bhadrakali, and is near a tropical forest.

Kerala's shrines follow different customs of worship, such as placing huge, tall brass lamps to ward off the evil spirits in the sacred circles that are under the power of the goddesses.

STORIES IN STONE

Sculpture is one of the oldest plastic arts known to man. Wondering how working with stone or wood can be called a plastic art? Plastic art is an art form in which you work with a material that can be carved, moulded or shaped. To plasticise means to mould and give form or shape to objects of different materials. Humans have expressed themselves through sculptures for centuries. In fact, it is said that the Venus of Hohle Fels, the oldest-known statue in the world, dates back to 38,000 years ago!

Temple sculptures are essentially stories carved in stone, and these stories are found across cultures and countries. The Greeks and Romans were famous for their monumental sculptures and grand temples for their gods, like the Temple of Zeus in Olympia, near Athens. Greek sculptures of the human form were considered both beautiful and sacred, whether they were of gods or ordinary mortals. Sculptors in ancient Greece used terracotta, marble and bronze, all of which were easily available in the Mediterranean region.

In northern Africa, the Egyptians built temples for their gods that were as massive as the ones they made for their pharaohs (kings). Bricks and stone, like sandstone, limestone and granite, were used in building temples. In South America, the Sun Temple at Coricancha in Peru was built by the Incas. It was constructed using special techniques of masonry, with sacred idols of the gods placed inside.

The first things you see when you set eyes upon the sky-high towers of an Indian temple are the sculptures. Indian temples are made from a variety of materials that are usually available around the area where the temple is located. The material could include terracotta, black granite, sandstone, red laterite stone, marble, wood or just rock faces. Sculptures are also made from metals like bronze and even wood. They are decorative and ornamental, and made by very skilled craftsmen, who were called *shilpis* (sculptors). The architects and master builders were called *sthapathis*.

Indian temple sculpture follows two kinds of styles: the Nagara style (sculptures found in temples and religious monuments in north India), and the Dravidian style (sculptures found in the temples of south India). North Indian temple towers, or *shikharas*, are tall with intricate carvings on them. In Odisha, Bengal and northeast India, tall towers called *deuls* are encircled with sculptural ornamentation. South Indian temple towers, called *gopurams*, are tall with flattened surfaces which are stacked with sculptures. The temple's mythology or story is seen sculpted on these *gopurams*.

Get up and close to the sculptures of the temple that you visit next time. You will observe a supernatural world of fairies and genies, gargoyles and ogres, gods and goddesses, humans and animals, birds and trees telling you magical stories of another time.

The Chariot of the Sun

Sun Temple, Konark, Odisha

After 12 long years, King Narasimhadeva of Kalinga finally lost patience and delivered an ultimatum to his chief temple architect, Bisu Maharana: 'The temple's finial has to be fixed by tomorrow – or else!'

The king's threat sounded ominous to Maharana and his 1,200 sculptors and craftsmen, who had been building a grand monument dedicated to the sun god for many years. However, the temple's finial, a decorative ornament on top of the *deul*, still needed to be completed and was proving to be a complicated task.

Dharmapada, Maharana's 12-year-old son, came to the site that day. Seeing his father looking distressed, he scrambled effortlessly to the top of the *deul* and fixed the finial. And then, he fell to his death from the top of the temple! Historians and storytellers still debate whether his death was a suicide or an accident. However, this tragic story apart, you can't help but feel awestruck while beholding the grand marvel of the Sun Temple at Konark. The splendid sculptures have made this temple a UNESCO World Heritage Site, and it holds the rightful honour as one of the best-sculpted temples of India.

The temple of the sun god Surya is sculpted to look like a giant ornamented chariot, and it faces east, so the first rays of the rising sun strike the main entrance. The architecture is symbolic, with the seven sculpted horses of the chariot representing the seven days of the week; the 12 pairs of wheels signifying the 12 months of a year; and the 24 wheels, which are sundials, pointing to the hours of a day!

The base and walls of the temple show scenes from the lives of the people of Kalinga – women cooking and washing their hair, men hunting, a holy man praying, a soldier going to war, bullock carts loaded with goods, people playing musical instruments, clowns and more. There are also sculptures of mythical birds, magical sea creatures and *surasundaris* (celestial beauties). The sculptures give us an idea of what life looked like in the past, and also tell us more about the beliefs and imagination of the people of that time.

Otherworldly Creatures

Lingaraja Temple, Bhubaneshwar, Odisha

One of the largest and oldest temples in Odisha, the Lingaraja Temple, is made of sandstone and laterite. It is also called Ekamra Shetra because legend has it that the lingam was found under a mango tree (*ekamra*). Shiva here is praised as Tribhuvaneshwara, or the lord of the three worlds, which is said to have given the city its name, Bhubaneshwar.

The 11th-century temple complex has sculptures of gods, humans and animals carved into the *deuls*, pillars and halls of the temple.

Udagajasingha (griffins) can be seen perched on the temple spire on sculpted elephant mounts. Griffins have the bodies of lions and the claws and wings of eagles. The *Nata mandir* or the dancing hall contains sculptures of *surasundaris*.

A Rocky Wonderland

Virupaksha and Vitthala Temples, Hampi, Karnataka

Legends often turn destinations into sacred sites, and legends of Shiva and Parvati visiting several places in India have turned many places into pilgrim centres. Once, Parvati turned into Pampa Devi and pursued Shiva to wed her on Earth. The place she followed him to was a rocky outcrop on the banks of the Tungabhadra River, where the boulders shone a brilliant sienna in the sunlight.

In this stark landscape, Shiva lived as a loner, and told Pampa that his life was hard and without comforts. Undeterred, Parvati too lived an ascetic lifestyle and performed penance here. Her resolve won the heart of the hermit god, and he wed her at Pampa Kshetra.

The oldest of all the temples here is the Virupaksha Temple, built for Shiva and Parvati, who is in the form of Pampa Devi. Over the centuries, the word Pampa perhaps turned to the Kannada word '*hampa*', and later to Hampi. Hampi has thousands of surviving ruins and granite temples that date back to the 14–16th centuries.

The Hampi temple complex has shrines, courtyards and open-pillared halls, a large community kitchen

Hoysala Wonders

The Hoysala dynasty is said to have created distinctive temple architecture styles found in Karnataka in the 11–14th centuries.

Belur and Halebidu are towns that are famous for the Chennakesava and the Hoysaleswara temples. The temples are world heritage monuments, thanks to their splendid sculptures.

The temples were made from soapstone, which is a soft material, so it was easy to sculpt fine details of jewellery, drapery and ornamental designs on them.

At the Chennakesava Temple, animals like elephants, lions, horses, swans, celestial nymphs, deities, demons, mythical figures like *yalis* and gargoyles are all sculpted to perfection on the walls. A signature Hoysala sculpture is the *salabhanjika*, a mythical maiden striking a pose before a sal tree.

The Hoysala temples were the first to have the names or signatures of the sculptors sculpted on the walls.

hall, a *gaja shala* (an eleven-domed elephant stable), sculpted lamp posts, pillars and shrines. The tiers of the Virupaksha temple tower are decorated with stone work. The Vitthala Temple, northeast of the Virupaksha Temple, has an extraordinary shrine sculpted in the shape of a chariot, called the Garuda shrine, after the celestial *vahana* of Vishnu.

One of the marvels of Hampi is a sculpture of Vishnu in a yogic pose in his Narasimha or lion avatar.

The Monk's Sanctuary

Vidyashankara Temple, Sringeri, Karnataka

The Sharada Peetham in Sringeri is a mutt, or a monastery, originally founded by Adi Shankara, an important 8th-century Hindu monk from south India. Vidyashankara was a follower of Adi Shankara, and the temple was built in his honour by two influential brothers, Harihara and Bukka, the founders of the Vijayanagara dynasty. The Vidyashankara Temple has many wonderful sculptures and showcases the features of Dravidian architecture.

The temple stands on a sculpted platform with six doorways. Twelve pillars signify the twelve signs of the zodiac. You can see stone columns with carved *yali*s; a *yali* is a mythical creature that's part lion, part horse, and part elephant, found in many south Indian temples. A stone ball rolls inside the roaring mouth of the *yali* in the temple.

The temple has a tomb of Vidyashankara, and the main shrine has a lingam with a richly sculpted tower over it.

Sculpted Saga

Kailasa Temple, Ellora, Maharashtra

The king was unwell and besieged by disease. The queen prayed to Shiva at Elapura to save him, and she promised to build a splendid temple if her prayers were answered. A miracle occurred, and the king soon regained his health.

The overjoyed queen ordered all the architects of the kingdom to begin work on a grand temple, but all of them refused. The area where the temple had to be built was dangerously rocky, and the earth around it needed to be excavated. The upset queen said she would fast to death until the architects agreed to start the construction.

The worried king had already sent his messengers around the kingdom to look for an architect, when a little-known architect named Kokasa came to the palace. He said he would do the deed. True to his word, in a week's time, he cut through the rock face, from top to bottom, inside the ground and even fixed a *shikhara* on it, prompting the queen to end her fast.

The 8th-century Kailasa Temple is part of 30 caves in this region. Cut out of rock and sculpted from a monolith (or a single large rock), the temple looks like it is located in a large pit and has four storeys from the plinth. It is made of black stone with sculptures of elephants and prowling lions adorning it. The best one is the sculpture of the demon king Ravana shaking Mount Kailasha.

The front walls of the temple that jut out of a massive rock have sculptures of dancers on them. Friezes, or panels of wall decoration, show war scenes, soldiers with bows and arrows, and warriors on chariots, elephants and magical creatures.

Rocky Labyrinth

The Elephanta Caves near Mumbai are a series of rock-cut caves that are UNESCO World Heritage Sites. On the rock face is a gigantic frieze of a three-faced meditating Shiva as the creator, preserver and destroyer of the universe. The rock-cut caves, which date back to 45–750 CE, have been carved into temples with pillars and walls with fantastic sculptures.

The Bird Town

Veerabhadra Temple, Lepakshi, Andhra Pradesh

The sculpted rocky boulders and hillocks of Lepakshi are filled with stories, folktales and local beliefs. One such story is that the town got its name from a character in the Ramayana. This is the spot where the celestial bird Jatayu, who was friends with King Dasharatha, was slain by Ravana.

Jatayu was an old bird, living alone on this rocky hillock. One day, he heard someone screaming, 'Rama, save me!' Jatayu became alert when he heard the name of his friend Rama being uttered. He looked up to see Sita crying for help from Ravana's flying chariot. He flapped his gigantic wings and soared upwards to rescue Sita. He valiantly battled Ravana mid-air, but the demon king cut off Jatayu's wings with his sword and felled the big bird. Rama and Lakshmana, in hot pursuit of Sita, found Jatayu bleeding to death. Even Rama's request, '*Le, pakshi*' or 'Arise, O bird' could not revive Jatayu.

But what makes Lepakshi a sacred site is the 16th-century Veerabhadra Temple. Veerabhadra was Shiva's mighty *bhoota gana*. For some devotees, Veerabhadra is a fierce form of Shiva himself. The temple complex was built by Virupanna, a treasurer who worked for a Vijayanagara king.

The Veerabhadra Temple has an unusual carved pillar hanging from the ceiling, which does not touch the floor. Visitors usually slide a piece of paper under it to check for themselves if the pillar touches the ground. Another dramatic touch is the enormous Nandi, wearing beautiful stone necklaces, sculpted from a single boulder.

The grand *kalyana mandapam*, or pillared wedding hall, has remained roofless and incomplete. Virupanna wanted the hall to be a place to commemorate the wedding of Shiva and Parvati at Pampa Kshetra. However, mischief-makers poisoned the king's ears saying that Virupanna had used money from the treasury to build this hall. The angry king commanded that Virupanna's eyes be gouged out, and a hurt Virupanna is said to have torn his own eyes out and smeared them on the wall. A ghastly red tint on the temple wall bears proof of this tale. The word '*lepakshi*' in Sanskrit also means 'smeared eyes'.

The most spectacular figurine at the Veerabhadra Temple is the gargantuan sculpture of the Nagalingam. This

lingam is encircled by the coils of a five-headed snake, its raised heads crowning the form of Shiva.

If you look closely, you will observe a crack at the base of the Nagalingam sculpture. No one knows if this crack appeared due to the stone weathering over centuries, but folklore has it that the sculptor had done such a good job so quickly that he earned the envy of other master *shilpis*. Some say the jealous sculptors cast an evil eye on this masterpiece, while others say they tried to ruin it and a mysterious crack appeared at the base overnight. But the sculpture is still a magnificent sight!

A Wedding to Remember

Meenakshi Amman Temple, Madurai, Tamil Nadu

It is said that the goddess Parvati was in such raptures when she laid eyes on Madurai from the heavens that Shiva shook his matted hair and shed ambrosia (*madhuram*) all over it. And that is how the charming city of jasmine blossoms earned its name as the city of nectar, or Madurapuri. Parvati then sped down to Earth, asking Shiva to meet her in Madurai at the right time, so they could marry. She was born as the warrior princess Meenakshi (the name means 'the one with the fish-shaped eyes') in the then-king's palace in Madurai.

Myths apart, the 16th-century temple showcases perfect sculptural art as described in the *Shilpa Shastras*, the ancient Hindu manuals on the science of arts and crafts. The tallest *gopuram* is 170-feet high and the towers are sculpted with hundreds of mythological stories. The Meenakshi Amman Temple has 14 *gopurams*, or tiered towers, forming a temple city square. The temple has unending corridors,

The Great Living Chola Temples

For sheer sculptural grandeur and awesome architecture visit the 11th-century temples of the Brihadeshwara Temple in Thanjavur, the Airavatesvara Temple in Darasuram and the Brihadisvara Temple in Gangaikonda Cholapuram. These medieval temples, in and around Thanjavur, were built by emperors Rajaraja Chola, Rajaraja Chola II and Rajendra Chola respectively.

The sculptures on the walls of these temples are social commentaries on the lifestyle of the people, the artists and poets. And to show that the king was touched by divinity himself, a sculpted tableau shows Shiva tying the regal turban at the coronation of Emperor Raja Raja Chola on the walls of the Big Temple.

a *killikoodu mandapam* (hall of sculpted parrots), *kalyana mandapam* (wedding hall), a pond blessed by Shiva for 'golden lotuses' to bloom, and a hall for Tamil Sangam poets to meet and compose beautiful verses.

And yes, Shiva did keep his promise. He shed his leopard skin and garland of skulls, and turned up in the finest silks and jewels to wed his beloved Meenakshi. A sculpted panel in the temple shows him as Sundareswarar, or Mr Handsome, with Vishnu placing the hand of his sister, Meenakshi, in Shiva's at the wedding.

The Lair of Dacoits

Bateshwar Temple, Morena, Madhya Pradesh

The Chambal River Valley was once famous for being the stomping ground of dangerous dacoits. But that's not all it is famous for. Located in the ravines of this valley, close to the hills near the town of Morena, is an area that looks like a plate of broken biscuits from afar in the white heat of the sun. When you come a little closer, you will see that it is scattered with some 200 temples. The main temple is dedicated to Shiva, and he is called Bhuteshwar here, or the lord of ghosts. The temple itself is known as the Bateshwar Temple. The other temples here are dedicated to Vishnu, Shakti and Hanuman. These otherwise silent temples are inhabited by wild peacocks and parakeets, whose loud calls pierce the air with their eerie music.

The 10th-century temples lay weathered by age and in ruins when archaeologists stumbled upon them as late as the 1920s. From then on, teams of archaeologists have worked to assemble the broken pieces of the temples and pillars, and restore them to a semblance of what they must have been. It is said that local dacoits of the area helped the archaeological team put the debris together and assemble them to make the temples. The result of their continuing work is a remarkable group of sandstone temples with exquisite sculpted towers, pillars and carved deities standing amidst the wild terrain.

Terracotta Tales

Shyam Rai Temple, Bishnupur, West Bengal

Terracotta is a type of burnt clay brick that is bright red in colour. In the 17th and 18th centuries, there was a flurry of temple building with terracotta in the town of Bishnupur in West Bengal. These striking red temples stand on elevated platforms and have unique architectural features like vaulted ceilings with a *shikhara* on top.

What is most extraordinary about these temples are the sculpted terracotta panels along the ceilings, walls and pillars of the temples, with minute ornamentation. The Bishnupur temples are predominantly dedicated to Vishnu and his different avatars. The recurring themes on the terracotta panels of other temples like Jor Bangla, Madan Mohan and Rasmancha in Bishnupur are from the Ramayana, Mahabharata, *Krishna Purana* and *Raslila*.

Talking Stones

Bhoramdeo Temple, Kabirdham, Chhattisgarh

On the banks of the Sakri River in Chhattisgarh, by a forest of bamboo, sal and tropical trees, there is a stunning temple complex. The Gonds, the tribal inhabitants of this area, venerate Shiva as Bhoramdeo, a tribal deity.

The temples were built between the 10th and 12th centuries by the serpent-worshipping Nagavanshi Rajput rulers of this region. Built with a mix of black granite and ochre sandstone, the colours of the temple blend naturally into their forested surroundings. The temple's architecture is unique in that it has a lot of carved images on its exterior walls. The towers are tightly packed with niches that have carved ornamental sculptures of deities like Vishnu, Ganesha and Parvati.

There are also sculptures of animals, birds, plants, celestial creatures, and elegant patterns on the borders. The doorpost to the sanctum sanctorum has carved statuettes of the river goddesses Ganga and Yamuna.

Sorceresses in Stone

Chausath Yogini Temple, Morena, Madhya Pradesh

Atop a hill in a city called Morena, there is an 11th-century temple with 64 mysterious sculpted women, called *yoginis*.

According to folklore the *yoginis* were sorceresses with capabilities to enchant and ensnare. There are many *yogini* temples in Odisha, Madhya Pradesh, Uttar Pradesh

and other places. These powerful women were said to be capable of wizardry. They knew 64 special arts (listed in ancient Hindu texts), from mathematics to magic, music to sorcery. And that's why the number 64 is associated with them.

The temple's architecture is grand, and, unlike other regular temples, it has no tower or roof! It is believed this allows the *yoginis* to fly in and out, like witches, over the roofless temple. The temple is circular, with pillars, 64 chambers and open halls. The inner circle is a round courtyard built with golden-yellow sandstone. In this temple, Shiva presides over these *yoginis*. While the chambers along the circular temple are shrines for Shiva, the *yoginis* are seen as part of these shrines.

It is said that this temple in Madhya Pradesh was the inspiration for the circular architecture of the Indian Parliament building in New Delhi.

A Swimming Pool for the Sun

Sun Temple, Modhera, Gujarat

An 11th-century Sun Temple in Gujarat flanks the grand Rama *kund*, a rectangular, stepped temple tank, with over 100 shrines for gods and three main shrines for Shiva, Vishnu and Ganesha, with sweeping steps leading to it.

The temple complex was built during the golden age of the Solanki dynasty, whose kings were *Suryavanshi*, or sun worshippers. An assembly called *sabha mandap* in the complex has 12 sculpted forms of Aditya, another name for Surya. These carvings show the sun during the 12 months of the year.

Epics and figures of gods, goddesses, celestial creatures and plants are carved on the pillars and rocks, and when the sun slants its rays on the sandstone monument, it glows golden in the light.

The Sea Rock's Story

Shore Temple, Mamallapuram, Tamil Nadu

Sea-faring Europeans like Marco Polo who landed in the little town of Mamallapuram in the Bay of Bengal in the 13th century called the temples they saw there the Seven Pagodas (as many shrines in the Orient were called by Europeans). Today only one of these 7th-century Pallava temples still stands, dramatically rising against the azure sky, flanked by the foaming sea, better known as the world-famous Shore Temple. (The others are believed to have been submerged under the sea over centuries of floods and storms.)

Mamallapuram, or Mahabalipuram, is named after the mythical king Bali, who was Prahalada's grandson. The Shore Temple was built by the Pallava emperor Narasimhavarman II.

A row of sacred bulls sculpted out of granite are seated along a wall in the compound of the temple. There are also groups of sculptures scattered around the complex, including a carved lion, which is a monolith (sculpted out of a single piece of rock). Decorated with sculptures of Shiva, Parvati, Ganesha, Skanda and Durga, the temple's towers have tiers of deities and a crowning top.

Pallava Architecture

Built between 600–700 CE, the Kailasanathar Temple is the oldest temple monument in Kanchipuram, which is some 60 km from Mamallapuram. The temple has 58 shrines dedicated to Shiva and was built by the Pallavas, whose signature architectural style can be spotted in both Mamallapuram and Kanchipuram. The Kailasanathar Temple is said to be the blueprint for temple architecture in Tamil Nadu. Mythical creatures, sculptures of gods and animals, long, pillared corridors and carved towers dot the temple complex.

Shiva's Happy Home

Bhuleshwar Temple, Pune, Maharashtra

Shiva may be famous for his fierce temper, but in the Bhuleshwar temple he is called the 'innocent god' or Bhola

Eshwar (Bhuleshwar), one who is easily pleased by the affection of his devotees. It is said that the spot where this temple stands, atop a hill, is where Parvati danced before Shiva and made him endlessly happy. The shrine is believed to have been built by the Pandavas for the happy lord. There are many sculptures of dancing goddesses on the walls to mark this legend.

This temple is built of dark stone, or black asphalt, with stacks of sculptures on the pillars, wall and towers. Scenes from the Mahabharata and the Ramayana are sculpted on the walls. A rare idol of Ganesha's female form as Vinayaki can be seen here. The sculptures of seven mother goddesses called Saptamatrika and a sculpture of Goddess Chamundi in the company of a scorpion can also be found here.

The Temple Architect

Ramappa Temple, Warangal, Telangana

Temples are usually named after gods and goddesses, but a 13th-century temple in south India has an unusual name. Sponsored by the Kakatiya king Ganapati Deva, the Shiva temple is known as Ramappa Temple after the architect who built it. It is perhaps the only temple in India named after its designer.

Unlike other temples of its time, the Ramappa Temple was built using an unusual combination of bricks and black granite. Bricks were not popular for temple building then. The temple stands on an elevated platform, and has numerous carvings and sculptures along its pillars and walls. A large Nandi sculpture stands in front of the Nandi *mandapam*. The statues of dancing nymphs and musicians inspired an ancient dance form called Perini Shivatandavam in this temple.

The Lakeside Temple

Jagdish Temple, Udaipur, Rajasthan

A gleaming white 17th-century temple stands in beautiful contrast to the blue sky of Udaipur, the city of lakes and palaces, in Rajasthan. With three tiers, the temple, built mainly of marble, is the largest in the city. Two huge sculpted elephants flank the entrance, and you will find pillared halls with detailed carvings and finely carved ceilings inside. There are over 50 pillars with exquisite carvings found here. The spire has sculptures of dancing women, musicians, elephants and soldiers riding horses. The main shrine is elegantly carved and houses a deity of Jagdish, or Vishnu with four arms.

The Lord from the North

Mahadeva Temple, Vaikom, Kerala

The temple architecture and sculpture in Kerala is unlike elsewhere in India. The architecture is influenced by natural elements, like heavy monsoons and tropical summers, so the temples have red terracotta-tiled, sloping roofs. The

space within the temple is designed in accordance to the rules of both Shilpa Shastra (sculptural rulebook) and Vastu Shastra (design and layout rulebook). The abundance of forests in Kerala has yielded timber for temple building and sculptures. The rafters and beams of temple roofs are carved, and the temples are, thus, a mix of stone and timber, giving them an elegant look.

The Mahadeva Temple at Vaikom has huge pillars in white lime with a towering red-tiled roof. The walls are splashed with figures in bright colours from the Ramayana, and the inner roof has sculptures of the heroes from the epic.

Sculptural Mix

The Padmanabhaswamy Temple in Thiruvananthapuram is a fantastic example of the Dravidian and Kerala styles of architecture. The *ottakkal mandapam* (hall carved out of a single boulder) in front of the main shrine is made out of a single granite boulder. The ceilings have remarkable wooden carvings on the beams and pillars. Sculptures of nymphs holding lamps, Nataraja, mythical beasts, serpents and tortoises can be found here.

Mountain Magic

Baleshwar Temple, Champawat, Uttarakhand

Built by the Chand dynasty between the 10th and 12th centuries, the Baleshwar Temple, dedicated to Shiva, is today surrounded by drab modern residential buildings in Champawat.

But when you enter the complex and take a closer look, it transports you to an antique land and time with its impressive shrines, walls and panels bearing carvings of designs and deities. A mix of sandstone and black granite makes the temple look like it's both in light and shade. The cupolas or domes are in light-coloured sandstone and the pillars are in black granite, covered with artistic carvings.

The Shiva lingam in the main shrine is called Baleshwar, and the temple has shrines for Shiva as Ratneshwar and Champawati Durga.

A Sculpted Heaven

Kopeshwar Mandir, Kolhapur, Maharashtra

Shiva's wrath was destroying the world! His darling wife, Sati, had just thrown herself into a sacrificial fire as her father, Daksha Prajapati, had humiliated Shiva.

The Earth trembled and shook as Shiva was hopping mad. The gods of heaven called him 'Kopeshwar Mahadev' or the 'almighty god of wrath' and beseeched Vishnu to soothe Shiva's anger. Vishnu sped to the spot by the river Krishna at Kolhapur where Shiva heaved in frenzy.

'Do not destroy the world in the name of Shakti who gives life on Earth,' Vishnu pacified Shiva, as the gods watched.

The sculptures of the Kopeshwar Mahadev temple bring this legend to life. Sculptures of Shiva's sons, Ganesha and Karthikeya, Indra, the god of war, Yama, the god of death, and the other gods and goddesses who were witness to Shiva's fury are carved in great detail on the temple's pillars and walls. The holy trinity of Brahma, Vishnu and Shiva are also engraved in this temple. Striking sculptures of elephants are carved on the base of the structure as if holding up the temple with their might.

Stand in the *swarg mandap* or the hall of heaven in Kopeshwar Mandir and look up. It is a sculpted tower with a round roofless ceiling. As you look up and see the clouds circle in the sky, it's hard not to believe that the heavens themselves have opened up!

SACRED SKILLS

Before written script and language evolved, humans used drawings and paintings to communicate with one another. Rocks and the walls of caves would be the canvas, while smoked sticks, charcoal, pieces of metal, shark teeth or hard shells were the art materials. The early humans drew figures of what they saw around them – boars, bison, deer, giant serpents, elephants, horses, fish, turtles and even scenes of rituals and dancing.

The tools may have been crude and the drawings rough, but this is valuable evidence of life in prehistoric times. The rock shelters at Bhimbetka, for instance, bear evidence of prehistoric ritual dances, battles and animals. And all of this was drawn 30,000 years ago! Archaeologists (scientists who study the past) have concluded that Bhimbetka could have been named after a warrior deity called Bhima, worshipped by the tribal folk of this region. Legends also say that the great warrior Bhima of the Mahabharata had hidden there when the Pandava princes lived in the jungles, for they were being hunted by their wicked cousins, the Kauravas. The wall art here includes figures now considered to be Shiva, Ganesha and a mother goddess.

Temples across India have always encouraged art. For centuries now, murals (paintings on rock or stone walls and ceilings), art on palm leaves, papier mâché, textiles, exquisite metal crafts and other handicrafts have been made by artisans who lived around the temples. Much of the religious art, until date, is inspired by the deities and the legends of the gods and goddesses of temple towns.

Whenever we visit a temple, it is important that we observe the art and crafts in its surroundings – for the art in each temple has a story to tell.

Kali's Sacred Souvenir

Kalighat Patachitra – Kalighat Kali Mandir, Kolkata, West Bengal

The lanes around most temples in India have shops that sell holy offerings. You would have seen flowers, fruits, sandalwood paste, areca nuts, turmeric roots, vermilion, sacred ash, *rudraksha* beads, souvenirs like brass, silver and earthen lamps, and blessed charms and idols of gods on sale in these shops.

A walk around the streets of the Kalighat Kali Mandir in Kolkata will show you many shops selling all of these, but you'll also see a special craft that is very famous here – hand-painted artworks of gods and goddesses called Kalighat *patachitra*.

Patachitra became famous in the 19th century, when village artists called *patua*s, or painters of cloths, engaged in folk arts and crafts. Many of them came to the big city of Kolkata to earn a living. They painted on cloth, which was prepared using a white paste made of lime and chalk, and sometimes with a mix of resin to give it a leathery finish. These cloths are called *pata*s; hence, the name *patachitra*. The artists draw the figures in ink and the illustrations are filled with colourful pigments from natural sources like vegetables, flowers, minerals and stones.

These artists would go to public squares or stand outside temples to sell their artworks. They would display

Yikes! Urine as Painting Material

Did you know that the bright yellow colour used in Indian paintings, like miniatures and *patas*, are believed to be produced from dried cow urine? At one time (in the 16–19th centuries CE), farmers would feed cows only mango leaves, because that helped the creatures produce dark yellow urine, which was then collected and dried in the sun, before being rolled into balls in parts of north India. It was even exported to Europe, where famous painters used 'Indian yellow' in their artworks.

their paintings, which depicted Shiva, Vishnu, Durga, Kali and other gods and goddesses, scenes from Tulsidas's Ramayana, the *Shiva Purana* and the *Shakti Purana*. These artists would also sing hymns and kirtans about the themes in their art.

The most enduring images of the *pata* are always of Kali or Durga, the resident of Bengal's most powerful temple, which is 200 years old. The temple is a *Shaktipeeth*, a place where Parvati's toe fell when Shiva danced the dance of destruction. The deity of Kali inside the temple is made of a large black stone, believed to be a sacred fossil.

Gods of Clay

Idol makers – Dhakeswari Mata Mandir, Kolkata, West Bengal

The Dhakeswari Mata Mandir stands on the eastern bank of the Hooghly River. Here, Goddess Katyayani Mahishasuramardini, seated on a lion, is the presiding deity. The idol is said to have been brought from Dhaka, Bangladesh, and hidden in a jungle nearby. Hence, the deity is known as Dhakeswari (the goddess from Dhaka or, in Bengali, the goddess who was hidden).

What cannot be hidden, however, is the neighbourhood near the temple, called Kumortuli, where many potters and clay idol makers live and work. They make grand idols of the goddess Durga, and sweeping tableaus of Durga, Lakshmi, Saraswati, Ganesha and Karthikeya.

The transformation of these grey, plain clay idols into colourful and beautiful figures of gods and goddesses is almost magical to watch. These are then placed in various pandals across the country during the Durga Puja festivities.

Epic Weaves

Baluchari Saris – Char Bangla Temple, Murshidabad, West Bengal

The village of Baluchar in Baranagar stands on the banks of River Bhagirathi in Murshidabad. It is famed for the terracotta panels of the 18th-century Char Bangla Temple, built by the local ruler Rani Bhavani. The terracotta panels portray scenes from the two great epics, the Ramayana and the Mahabharata.

The temple has shrines for Shiva and sculptures of Rama, Lakshmana and Ravana on its walls, as well as scenes from *Krishna Lila* and Goddess Kali's battle against demons.

In those days, the royals and nobles who built these temples were also patrons of art, and wore the very best jewels and silks. It is not surprising then that the Murshidabad silks, called Baluchari, are famous for depicting the panels of these temples. The silk saris, traditionally in white, red, yellow and blue, have borders and motifs of scenes from the Ramayana, *Krishna Lila* and the *Shakti Purana* beautifully woven into them.

Sacred Plant Craft

Sholapith – Sarbamangala Temple, Bardhaman, West Bengal

Quietly flow the rivers Damodar and Banka through the district of Bardhaman, on whose fertile banks stands the 18th-century Sarbamangala Temple. This *Shaktipeeth* houses the shrine of Goddess Durga, a deity with 18 arms. With its blend of terracotta and lime-plaster architecture, and honeycomb-like *deul*, it is not only one of the most beautiful temples in Bengal, but also one of the most important.

Bardhaman, among other places in Bengal, is famous for the religious craft of *sholapith*, or the Indian cork – a weed-like plant that grows in water and marshy land.

When the plant is dried, it yields a spongy, pristine white cellulosic matter. Artisans craft these into beautiful decorative objects, of which the face of Durga is the most special. Bengali brides and grooms too wear crowns made of *sholapith* on their wedding day, and these religious objects are commonly found in the temples.

The artisans using *sholapith* are called *malakars* or garland makers. The *Brahma Vaivarta Purana*, a Bhakti text, has a story to tell about this craft.

Lord Shiva was on his way to the Himalayas to wed Parvati, and he wanted to wear a crown as white as the moon. The divine sculptor Biswakarma saw the *shola* growing in the marshes of Bengal, and crafted a garland and crown for Shiva. Since then, the craftspeople have been called the descendants of Biswakarma and *malakars*.

Traditional *malakars* usually begin making the grand Durga Puja idols by offering a special prayer to Shiva before they start their work.

Prayer Towel Craft

Gamosa – Namghar, Assam

An iconic motif from Assam is the *gamosa*, a handwoven piece of white cloth with a striking red embroidered border. The Assamese use it for all formal and cultural occasions as an auspicious textile. Bihu dancers wear it around their waists or as head bands, and elders are gifted the *gamosa* on festive occasions.

The one place where the *gamosa* attains a higher station is at the *namghar*, or Vaishnava prayer houses across

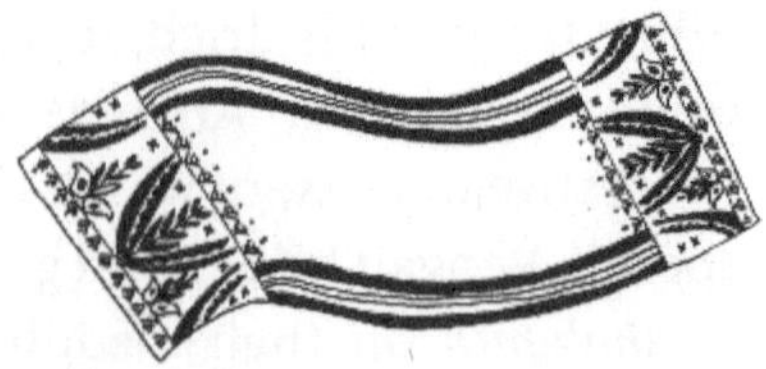

Assam. *Namghar*s have a shrine called *monikut* for the deity. This resembles a hill made of tiny steps with the idol inside. The steps are often adorned with the *gamosa*. The holy book *Bhagavata Purana* by the 15th-century saint Srimant Sankardeva is often placed in *namghar*s on a *gamosa*.

Prayers on *Pattachitra*

Pattachitra – Jagannath Mandir, Puri, Odisha

Odisha has a rich culture of arts and crafts. In the fifth century, artists painted scenes of Krishna or Jagannath, and from the *Vishnu Purana*s on temple walls. They are called murals and they are found in the temples of Puri, Bhubaneshwar and Konark. It is said that sculptors would often double up as mural painters in the temples.

On occasions when the priests would shut the doors of the shrine for any ritual cleaning or to spruce up the idols, the paintings of Lord Jagannath, Subhadra and Balarama, on the outside walls of the shrine, would be worshipped by priests and devotees.

The village of Raghurajpur near Puri is especially famous for its *pattachitra* artists. The artists making temple murals realized that *patta*, or cloth, and even palm fronds worked as mediums for their artwork. While the *patachitra* artwork in Bengal has simple lines and figures painted against a white backdrop, the *pattachitra* art of

Odisha is marked by small figures and with elaborate details, designs and patterns on the backdrop.

Thus was born the popular Odisha *pattachitra* painting. Its themes echoed the tales of the temples around which the artists would sell their works. The *Dasavatara*, or the ten avatars of Vishnu, *Krishna Lila*, *Shakti Purana*, the temple deities and folktales from the region are popular themes for *pattachitra* artists.

Odisha's *pattachitra* artworks are full of geometrical and floral designs on the background, against which figures of gods and goddesses are painted. The faces, often seen as profiles, have well-defined features with slanted eyes, sharp noses and full lips. The paintings have colourful borders filled with designs and patterns that help to make the main painting stand out.

Gods on Walls

Shekhawati painting – Raghunathji Mandir, Sikar, Rajasthan

As the sun's harsh glare sears the sandy dunes of the Thar Desert, the ochre landscape is brightened by some remarkable murals on the walls of havelis, forts and temples in Shekhawati, or the Garden of Shekha.

The Shekhawati region in north Rajasthan is named after the 15th-century ruler Rao Shekha. As you walk down the dusty streets, you cannot miss the many stories from the Ramayana, *Dasavatara*, *Shakti*, *Shiva* and *Krishna Puranas* and *Raslila* painted on the buildings here.

These murals are painted with bright colours made of natural pigments using plant dyes and mineral powders. The murals are dotted with gods and goddesses, kings and queens, animals, birds, fruits and flowers drawn by hand.

The Raghunathji Mandir is a temple locally known as Bara Mandir. It has haveli-like features, with high walls and onion-like domes. Devotees pray at this 19th-century temple to Raghunath or Rama. It has murals of gods, the kings of Sikar and even an Englishman, who was a keen astronomer.

The other temples in Sikar, like the tenth-century Harshnath Temple, Madan Mohan Temple, Govindji and Jeen Mata Mandir also have beautiful murals in them.

The Great Indian Natural Dyes

India is famous for producing colours from many natural plant and animal sources. These were used for dyeing textiles and pigments for paintings on cloth, walls and wood, found in many temples across India. Here are some natural dyes, some of which are used even today.

indigo plant - blue
lapis lazuli - brilliant blue
night jasmine, turmeric - yellow
manjista or Indian madder/pomegranate rind - red
safflower - orange
lamp oil residue or soot - black

Sacred Wall Hanging

Pichhwai painting – Shrinathji ki Haveli, Nathdwara, Rajasthan

Nathdwara is a temple town in Rajasthan, which is famous for its depiction of Lord Shrinathji, or Krishna as a young boy.

The legend of Govardhan Giridhara is celebrated in songs, poems and sculptures. Still, nothing is more popular than *pichhwai*, a unique style of painting, usually portraying the deity of Nathdwara, which is found in wall hangings, murals and even printed art these days.

According to the *Krishna Purana*, even as a boy, people noted that Krishna was wise beyond his years. Once, he found the farmers and cowherds in his village busy preparing for a ritual sacrifice to Indra, the lord of the heavens. He explained to them that doing one's duty was a better way of pleasing the god than offering sacrifices. The villagers saw wisdom in Krishna's words and went about their work again.

An angry Indra released rain and thunder and flooded the homes and farms of the villagers. When they cried for help, Krishna lifted the Govardhan mountain (*go* means cow and *vardhan* means nurturer) with his little finger, offering the cowherds and their cattle protection from the rains, keeping them safe and dry.

The kings of Mewar in the 17th century were devotees of Krishna, and built the temple for the divine deity of Shrinathji, depicting the Govardhan miracle. In fact, the temple is built in the style of a haveli. Locals call it Shrinathji's haveli, instead of a mandir, to cement the belief that Krishna reigns as king in the hearts of the devotees of Nathdwara.

The deity of Shrinathji is a cherubic Krishna, with a twinkling diamond pin on his dimpled chin, chubby cheeks and half-closed eyes, a little smile dancing on his lips. His right arm is akimbo, and his left is held up to suggest the balancing of Govardhan.

The Shrinathji idol is sculpted out of a large slab of black stone with carved motifs of sages, beasts and birds on the sides. The deity is dressed in glittering scarfs and silks, and twinkling pearl and gemstone necklaces cover him from top to bottom. On his head rests a delicate turbaned crown topped with a peacock feather.

This image is unforgettable for even those who have not visited this temple because of the *pichhwai* artists who have made paintings of Nathdwara's Shrinathji famous.

The word *pichhwai* means 'a wall hanging at the back', as these devotional wall hangings would hang behind the temple deity as a backdrop.

The *pichhwai*s are highly decorated, with the main figure of Shrinathji set against a background of designs, patterns, colours, and plant and creeper motifs that look like lace work. *Pichhwai*s were traditionally painted on walls or cloth, but in recent times, artists have started using paper. They were originally painted using natural pigments and colours.

It is not an exaggeration to say that in Nathdwara, the *pichhwai* is as important a devotional offering to Shrinathji as flowers, fruits and sweets.

Sacred Scrolls

Phad Paintings – Lok Devta Pabuji Mandir, Kolu, Rajasthan

In the 14th century, there lived a folk hero named Devnarayan, called Pabuji by his followers, in Kolu, a village near Jodhpur in Rajasthan. Pabuji was special as, unlike his siblings, his mother was not a mortal but a heavenly creature. This gave him magical powers.

Pabuji's bravery and kindness soon made him a Rajput folk hero. Praises of his bravery and his ability to work miracles and protect animals were sung as songs, called *Pabuprakasa*, by the wandering nomads of the deserts called Rabaris, who considered him their god. Pabuji is believed to have cured children and women of illnesses; and the Bhopas, another wandering tribe in Rajasthan, pray to him to protect their cattle.

The Lok Devta Pabuji Mandir is a small temple in Kolu, the village Pabuji was born in, where prayers are offered to him.

While he remains a local folk deity, Pabuji is famous across India thanks to the *phad*, or scroll paintings of Rajasthan.

These large scrolls are usually painted in bright colours, such as reds, yellows and greens, on long canvases or heavy cloth, called *phad*, that are sometimes up to 30 feet in length. Called devotional scrolls, they are filled with figures of kings and soldiers engaged in battle, or they depict processions led by horses and elephants, or festive occasions, with Pabuji towering over all of them as the main figure.

Priests and elders of the nomadic Bhopa tribe are known to paint these lengthy scrolls. They carry them around, halt at public spaces, and sing songs of Pabuji's miracles holding them aloft. These scrolls have been showcased in museums across the world, winning acclaim for their detailed workmanship.

Sita's Homespun Art

Madhubani Painting – Kapileswarsthan Mandir, Mithila, Bihar

Sita, the heroine of the Ramayana, is also called Maithili, as she was the daughter of Janaka, ruler of the kingdom of Mithila (in present-day Bihar). The famous folk art of Bihar from this region is called Mithila painting, though it is better known as Madhubani art. Legend has it that King Janaka commissioned village artists to paint the walls of his palace during his daughter's wedding to Lord Rama, and that is how Madhubani art is said to have been born.

Mythology apart, the art form is said to have been practised from the 14th century onwards by women who painted the walls of their homes.

They were also painted during special occasions, such as weddings, Holi, Kali Puja or Surya Shasti.

Bright and cheerful, Madhubani paintings are filled with images of Rama, Lakshmana and Sita, apart from other gods like Krishna and Radha, Surya, Shiva, Parvati and Ganesha, set against colourful plants, creepers, flowers and geometric patterns.

While Bihar has many temples, the Kapileswarsthan Mandir for Shiva and the Ram Janki Mandir are the most famous, and draw a number of devotees. But the gods can be found here beyond the confines of the temples – in shops and homes, drawn with such delightful simplicity that they endear themselves to both the devotee and the lover of art.

Marble Gods

Marble Craft – Chausath Yogini Temple, Bhedaghat, Madhya Pradesh

The relationship between nature and man is special. Bhedaghat's geographical location offers a unique raw material for producing religious handicrafts. In this town, in Madhya Pradesh's Jabalpur district, the Narmada River flows past a rare rock formation called marble rocks. These massive marble gorges jut into the water, creating a unique riverscape.

The marble here has a smooth and supple texture, like soapstone, and is rich in magnesium and comes in various shades of white, blue and brown. It is no surprise that this place is famous for crafting idols made from this marble.

The stones washed ashore and the massive marble hillocks provide the raw material for craftsmen to sit by the ghats of the river and chisel idols of Ganesha, Shiva and Parvati. Over here, you can not only watch the artisans at work, but you can also buy the idols directly from them.

What brings devotees to this spot is the Chausath Yogini Temple. This majestic temple is different as it is located on top of a hillock and houses Shiva and Parvati in the main shrine with images of the celestial yoginis sculpted around pillars and walls.

Sacred Games

Ganjifa Cards – Ranganathaswamy Temple, Srirangapatna, Karnataka

Playing cards are amongst the most popular table games in the world. A set of cards, often rectangular in shape, with various numbers on one side and figures of kings, queens and symbols on the other, are used as the material for the game.

Playing cards are distributed in different combinations and numbers among a group and played. The players wage money on their cards and the winners often walk away from the table with a rich stack of money. Cards have also been used for supernatural predictions by astrologers.

Who knew that this game could give way to a beautiful craft form that travelled all the way from Persia to the south Indian temple town of Srirangapatna!

Ganjifa comes from the Persian word for playing cards and is known as *kreedapatra* in ancient Sanskrit literature. There are records of royals and aristocrats across Gujarat,

Odisha and Karnataka playing *kreedapatra*.

The Mughal rule in Karnataka saw this royal game gain popularity in the 16th century. The original cards were round in shape and made of wood, cloth and paper, and they had Persian designs painted with vegetable dyes. These cards were mostly played among the royals and wealthy classes. The Mysuru Wodeyar kings called the cards *devarapatra* or sacred cards, as they had colourful images of gods and goddesses painted on them.

The game is no longer played in modern times; but the art on the cards continues to charm people who hang them as decorative wall art today.

The majestic temple of Ranganathaswamy in Srirangapatna, near Mysuru, is a sacred site for Vishnu. Craftspeople in this region pay homage to Ranganathaswamy or Vishnu who remains a popular image painted on the Ganjifa cards. The ten avatars of Vishnu are a popular theme on the cards, as also are divine figures from the Ramayana, *Krishna Lila*, and Durga and Lakshmi.

A few dedicated craftspeople continue to paint the Ganjifa cards even today in and around Srirangapatna. This shows how art forms thrive under the shadow of these temples.

Gods on Glass

Mysore Painting – Chamundeshwari Temple, Mysuru, Karnataka

Mysuru is one of the most popular heritage cities in India. The name Mysuru comes from the word Mahishasura, the buffalo-headed demon who was killed by Goddess Durga after nine long days of battle. Durga towers over the city from atop the Chamundi Hills, where the grand Chamundeshwari Temple stands. It is believed that she vanquished the demon at this spot.

Goddess Chamundeshwari is the deity for the royal family of Mysuru, who host the grandest Dussehra festival in Karnataka from this temple.

In the 16th century, the Vijayanagara kingdom was plagued by battles and turmoil. The local painters, called *chitrakaras* in Kannada, moved around Karnataka for the sake of their safety. These talented artists – who settled in and around Mysuru, Srirangapatna and the Mandya region – received protection and patronage from the Wodeyar rulers, who were devotees of Goddess Chamundeshwari. The artisans excelled at painting murals on the walls of temples built by the kings of this region.

In the 17th and 18th centuries, this became a formal style of art under Krishnaraja Wodeyar. He founded the Mysore School of Art, and also wrote the *Sritattvanidhi,* a book that listed the styles of drawing gods and goddesses, the colour schemes and composition, and the designs of the paintings. The paintings were created on walls, wooden boards, and a specific kind of cloth, stiffened using paints.

The technique special to Mysore paintings is gesso work, which uses light gold foil to highlight them, giving the artworks a gilded touch. Luminous and curved forms of Radha, Rukmini and Satyabhama with Krishna, Balarama, and the goddesses Chamundeshwari and Durga are popular motifs found in Mysore paintings.

In recent times, artists have also begun painting on glass with gold pigments, making these magnificent paintings look even more grand.

Man's Best Friend

Channapatna Toys – Dog Temple, Channapatna, Karnataka

The town of Channapatna, near Bengaluru, is locally called 'the land of toys'. In this age of plastic dolls and toys, the Channapatna toys stand out, for they are made from the locally grown soft ivory wood tree. These natural toys are chiselled by hand and painted in bright colours. The town of Channapatna is filled with craftsmen, whose craft goes back to the times of Karnataka's famous 18th-century ruler Tipu Sultan, who supported and patronized this art form.

Made of soft wood, these delightful toys include trains, bobble heads, spinning tops, figures of temple priests, Nandi, infant Krishna, Vishnu, animals and birds. These toys are often used as Golu *gombe*, or dolls of the Golu, a festive display during Navaratri where clay and wooden idols of gods, goddesses and toys are exhibited on metal steps in homes.

In this land of toys stands a quirky temple called Nai Devasthana (Dog Temple), built in 2010 by a rich businessman. Idols of two canines, one brown and the other white, are housed in a kennel-like shrine.

The idols are garlanded and worshipped as guardian angels to ward off evil in the little town. Man's best friend has been elevated to the status of a god here, and the residents host a big festival every year celebrating these canine guardian angels.

The Raja–Rani Duo

Marapachi Bommalu – Srikalahasti Temple, Andhra Pradesh

On the banks of River Swarnamukhi, at the foothills of Tirumala Hills, is the stately temple of Srikalahasti, dotted with red wood and red sandalwood trees, and venerated as an important shrine for Lord Shiva.

In this temple, Shiva is a powerful deity, worshipped as the element of air. Once upon a time, Vayu, the god of wind, performed a severe penance to Shiva, as a lingam made of camphor, a forest product that releases a strong smell when it melts or burns. Pleased with his prayers, Shiva appeared before Vayu, and agreed to grant him anything he wanted. Vayu asked Shiva to bless him with a boon that allowed him to be present everywhere, as the wind that blows all over the world. Shiva agreed and the lingam that Vayu prayed to stands in the *Panchabhootha sthalam* of Srikalahasti, named thus as Shiva was the protector of both the divine serpent and the elephants of this wooded area.

Most devotees offer prayers at Srikalahasti before their trek uphill to Tirupati to worship Lord Venkateshwara. This town is also known for a famous red wood that is used by local craftspeople to make idols called *rakta bommalu* (blood dolls in Telugu as the wood yields a red paste when rubbed against stone) or *marapachi dampathi bommalu* (wooden dolls of a couple).

Panchabhootha Sthalam

Panchabhootha sthalam refers to five sacred sites for Shiva, the lord of the universe, in and around Tamil Nadu. In each sacred site, Shiva represents one of the five cosmic matters - air, water, earth, sky and ether or space. He is manifested as earth at the Ekambareswarar Temple in Kanchipuram; water at Jambukeswarar in Thiruvanaikaval; fire at Arunachalesvara Temple in Thiruvannamalai; air at Srikalahasti Temple in Srikalahasti, and as space at Nataraja Temple in Chidambaram.

The *dampati bommalu* (divine couple of a raja and rani), believed to be Tirupati's Venkateshwara and Padmavati, are auspicious dolls made of this red teakwood.

Toying with Gods

Kondapalli Bomma – Sri Kanaka Durga Temple, Vijayawada, Andhra Pradesh

Kondapalli is a busy industrial town in Vijayawada, best known for the crafts named after it. The town's craftspeople specialize in wooden toys made from a locally grown soft wood called *tellaponiki*, which are chiselled into toys and painted with vegetable dyes. To keep up with the times, these toys shimmer with enamel colours these days. Yet their charm remains undiminished with modernity.

The most common themes of Kondapalli toys are folk idols, farmers and their cattle, religious and royal processions on horses and elephants, and gods, like the ten avatars of Vishnu, all painted in bright colours.

Vijayawada is famous for these Kondapalli toys and also for the sacred Kanaka Durga Devi Temple that stands atop the Indrakeeladri Hill.

Once, Sage Indrakeela begged for a boon from Goddess Shakti to come to Earth and kill a demon who was troubling innocent people. The goddess took the form of Durga, the warrior avatar of Shakti, and vanquished the evil demon. Sage Indrakeela requested her to stay back and guard over the people in the Kanaka Durga Temple.

The Magic of Murals

Murals – Ettumanoor Mahadeva Temple, Kottayam, Kerala

Many temples of Kerala boast of incredibly grand, intricate murals. These murals sprang up in temples in the ninth century, with active encouragement and appreciation from the kings of Kerala.

The stark and clean lines of the temples are in direct contrast to these extraordinary murals, painted in brilliant reds, greens and yellows.

The themes of these murals are often from the Ramayana, Mahabharata and the *Shiva Purana*. They feature figures of Krishna, Vishnu, Shiva and magical creatures like *yakshis*. These divine beings seem to float against a backdrop of curly designs and motifs, thickly set like a carpet. They also resemble the designs of the Theyyam ritual masks.

These murals follow a strict code of composition, colour and preparation. They are believed to be infused with magical qualities, as is explained in texts on art like *Chithrasoothram, Silparatna* and *Tantrasamuchaya*. The walls are prepared elaborately with lime and coconut water, and evened out with cotton fibre to create the perfect canvas for the murals.

While such murals are usually found in the palaces of the state, some of Kerala's sacred temples are also known for their grand murals. The Ramayana murals at the Vadakkunnathan Shiva Temple; Vishnu in *ananthasaiyanam,* or the reclining pose, in the Pallikurup Maha Vishnu Temple; and the murals at the Padmanabhaswamy Temple are the most famous.

The grandest mural in Kerala, however, is at the Ettumanoor Mahadeva Temple. It is an important Shiva *sthala*, considered one of the most sacred sites in Kerala.

The temple's highlights include the mural of *pradosha nritham* (the dance of Shiva at the auspicious hour of dusk). This majestic mural shows Shiva dancing on the demon of ignorance, within the circle of life, while serpents, gods, goddesses, *bhoota ganas*, *devas*, *yakshis* and other celestial creatures watch.

Brilliance in Bronze

Bronze Idols – Brihadeshwara Temple, Thanjavur, Tamil Nadu

If there is one major Indian artefact seen in many museums of the world, it is the medieval Chola bronze idol. While bronze idols were a highly developed craft in Tamil Nadu as early as the ninth century, they reached their zenith under the Chola kings, well into the 12th century, when they were used as processional deities in major temples.

Temples have a *garbha griha* (holy shrine), where the main deity, often made of granite, is placed for worship. The deity cannot be moved out, and hence prayers and worship are only offered in front of the shrine. In the olden times only priests, kings and royals were allowed to go near the shrine to offer prayers.

On festivals and auspicious days, it was important for the king to share the blessings of the god of the temple with all his subjects. For that purpose, the kingdom's skilled metal craftsmen fashioned a replica of the temple deity in bronze. The idol could then be taken out on the streets around the temple town in a *ratha* by the devotees. This allowed everyone to gather and worship, and have a darshan of the god. Thus, these bronze idols were also

The Lost-Wax Method

The Chola bronze idols were actually made of a mix of five metals – gold, silver, copper, iron and lead. They were made according to the details in *Shilpashastra*, the textbook on idol making. The idol would first be crafted out of beeswax, which was hollow inside. It would then be baked and hardened, after which the molten metal would be poured into the hollow figurine, filling all the nooks and crannies. Then, the mould would be dunked in cold water and the wax would chip away, leaving behind the dull yet perfect metal idol in all its beauty. Even today, there are craftsmen in Thanjavur who make these idols using this method, which is called the lost-wax technique.

called *utsava murthy* (processional idols). The large idols have holes at the base to insert poles and ropes to help carry them during processions.

The idols of Shiva and Parvati, Vishnu and his wife, Padmavati, Subrahmanya and his wives, Valli and Devasena, and even the Nayanmars and Alwars, or Saivite and Vaishnavite saints, are dressed in special jewels, silks and velvets. Crowns studded with gems adorn their heads and rich garlands hang from their necks as the processions are taken out.

The Brihadeshwara Temple in Thanjavur has inscriptions on its walls that mention that it had over 60 bronze idols of gods and goddesses in its vaults for the processions. While, for devotees, they remain idols to be worshipped, for art lovers, the perfection of form and grace and the majesty of these idols made by hand make them precious objects.

Gods in Gold

Thanjavur Paintings – Brihadeshwara Temple, Tamil Nadu

Thanjavur was an important site for the powerful kingdoms and dynasties of Tamil emperors. Even the Nayak kings of Vijayanagara and the Marathas left their footprints here. What the holy city of Varanasi was to north India, Thanjavur and the Big Temple were to the Tamils for hundreds of centuries.

The large murals on the walls of the Brihadeshwara Temple are easily identifiable by their chubby-faced gods and goddesses. Under Maratha rule, during the 16th century, a new art form became popular in the court of the king: Thanjavur painting. Painted with vegetable dyes on wooden plates were figures of gods and goddesses, the borders embellished with gold foil and gems, giving the painting a bejewelled look.

These costly pieces of art, birthed at this temple, were patronized by kings, royals and the merchant class.

Lighting Up the Temples

Nachiarkoil Brass Lamps – Nachiar Temple, Thirunarayur, Tamil Nadu

A striking vision of temple worship in Tamil Nadu is the variety of brass lamps that are lit in the dark shrine before the deity. These lights lend an enigmatic beauty to the deity in the shrine. The accompanying prayers, bells ringing, the smell of camphor and holy smoke from incense sticks add to the spirit of worship.

In a small village called Thirunarayur in Tamil Nadu, there is a temple that is a sacred site for Vishnu devotees, and the place is also famous for the hundreds of craftsmen who make brass lamps for ritual worship.

Devotees in rapture often call out the name of the god when these lamps are held aloft by priests before the deities, for the swaying flames are a form of worship.

The temple legend has it that a sage called Medhavi lived in this village and was an ardent Vishnu devotee. Once, while taking a bath in the River Cauvery, he found an image of Vishnu holding his discus with an idol of him in his Narasimha avatar. Medhavi built a shrine for the deities, and offered worship here. Goddess Lakshmi, meanwhile, came down to Earth and took the form of a young girl, and asked to stay in the sage's hermitage as his daughter. In Vaikunta, or Vishnu's heavenly abode, Lakshmi's absence was noted and he followed her down to Earth on Garuda, his half-kite, half-man mount.

Vishnu offered a darshan to the sage and requested that he be allowed to marry his beautiful daughter. The sage was awestruck to behold both Vishnu and Lakshmi, and said that he could not part with them. And so he built a temple for them.

South Indian brass lamps for temple worship are mostly made in this little village. Temple worship requires lamps of special sizes and designs, and these master craftsmen, called *pather*, have been making these lamps for hundreds of years.

It is said that the soft brown sand of the River Cauvery is ideal for making the mould for the lamps.

Now, the Nachiarkoil lamp is registered as a special craft, which shows the unique place it enjoys in India's arts and crafts. These lamps continue to illuminate temples, allowing devotees to worship the gods.

The Brilliant Gem

Temple Jewellery – Bhagavathy Amman Temple, Kanyakumari, Tamil Nadu

On the blackest of nights, a pious sailor, whose ship was tossed by the fury of the sea, called out to the goddess

Bhagavathy for help. Miraculously, a blue light twinkled from land, helping him to sail to the shore safely. Upon reaching the beach he found that it was not a lighthouse but the brilliant light from the diamond nose-pin of Goddess Kanyakumari, whose temple stands on the seashore, that had guided him to safety.

This tall tale has never gone out of its retelling, much like the doomed romance of the heavenly maiden and her groom, Shiva.

In the temple's shrine, the deity of Goddess Kanyakumari stands in the form of a young maiden, dressed in silk skirts and glittering jewels. She is said to be eternally waiting for Lord Shiva to come and wed her. For he had failed to turn up for their beachside wedding. And that was all due to the trick played by Narada, the clever and naughty sage.

You see, Kanyakumari was actually Parashakti, the goddess of supreme energy. The gods of heaven had sent her down to Earth to kill the wicked demon Banasura at this spot. Even Shiva, who was residing in the neighbourhood of Suchindram, did not recognize her as Shakti when he fell in love with her.

'Come to the tip of the land and let's wed by the beach at night, with the stars shining their light on us,' Kanyakumari told Shiva, who happily agreed.

Oops! That romantic wedding would ruin the plan of Kanyakumari morphing into Parashakti to kill Banasura on that very night, thought Narada.

He hatched a plan to stop the wedding and turned into a rooster and crowed loudly in Shiva's ear, waking him up at midnight. Confused into thinking that dawn had broken and the auspicious time for their wedding had gone, a dejected Shiva stayed back at the Suchindram temple.

Meanwhile, a disappointed Kanyakumari shed her wedding finery, transformed into Parashakti and turned to the job at hand and slayed Banasura that night.

After the battle, her pent-up fury died down and sadness washed over her.

Kanyakumari then walked up to the shore, heartbroken, yet full of hope, and decided to wait eternally for Shiva to come and wed her some day.

Deities in temples are usually adorned in brilliant gemstones and shining gold jewellery. Classical dancers also wear jewels that are modelled after the ones that adorn the temple idols. Hence the term temple jewellery.

A small neighbourhood called Vadasery, in Nagarcoil in Kanyakumari district, is the hub for hereditary artisans and goldsmiths who make temple jewellery. They design jewels that adorn temple deities and for Bharatanatyam dancers in Tamil Nadu to wear. Made of silver and coated in gold and studded with gemstones, these jewels look resplendent! Temple jewellery is also worn by Tamil brides on their wedding day, much like the divine maiden who stands in eternal wait for her groom in Kanyakumari.

DIVINE DANCES AND SONGS

Dance and music have been with us for a long, long time. Ancient civilizations used them, well before language was developed, to communicate with forces they didn't understand.

The Incas of South America worshipped the sun god with dance. The ancient Roman civilization had special dances – that mostly consisted of jumps and marches – to be performed during feasts and sacred rituals. The Acropolis in Greece would showcase dance and music as a form of storytelling. In Persia, ceramic shards and other findings show that dance and music were part of community celebrations.

Before religion as we know it came into being, early man would worship nature. The sun, moon, thunder and rain, and fierce creatures – both real and imaginary – were worshipped in many civilizations as they were still mysteries to humans. The Chinese civilization had dragon dances dedicated to the rain gods. The Egyptian civilization was famous for its temple dancers.

Closer home, the Indus Valley civilization's most famous symbol was the Dancing Girl. The prehistoric bronze sculpture is that of a dancer, one arm akimbo, the other resting on her thigh, striking a jaunty pose. Millennia later, the same posture can be found sculpted on the pillars and walls of many Indian temples.

In India, temples were the spaces where dance, poetry, music and the performing arts flourished. Most temples had stages or platforms, where performances were held before kings or noblemen.

Temples across India are linked to dance forms like Bharatanatyam, Kathakali, Odissi and Manipuri. Folk, tribal and street theatre performances were also hosted in and around famous temples and during festivals.

Similarly, temples are also synonymous with music. Poets and composers often wrote songs in praise of the temple deity, and their songs carried the names of the gods and temple towns.

Today, dance and music festivals are still held in many temple precincts, like the Mamallapuram Dance Festival near the Pallava Shore Temple in Tamil Nadu, the dance festival at the Sun Temple in Modhera in Gujarat and Tansen Samaroh in Gwalior, among many others. This speaks volumes of the continuing links between our temples and music and dance.

In no other country in the world can you find such a strong and continuing connection between music and dance forms and temples. Read on to find out how dances and songs composed about the gods and goddesses of these temples are performed even today in the 21st century.

The King of Dance

Chidambaram Nataraja Temple, Tamil Nadu

We know that gods have many forms, each of them vastly different from the other. Who would have thought that the serious, ascetic-like Shiva could also be the king of dance?

A temple in the small town of Chidambaram, in Tamil Nadu, is home to Nataraja (literally, the 'king of dance'). In fact, this is the only temple in the country where Shiva stands in the shrine not as a stone lingam, but as a brilliant Chola-era bronze idol in his avatar as the dancing Nataraja.

The sages Patanjali and Vyaghrapada once wanted to watch Shiva's *ananda thandavan* (dance celebrating the joy of life). They undertook a penance and when Shiva appeared before them, they requested him to perform this dance. Shiva said he would, when the time was right.

On an auspicious day, Shiva is said to have appeared on Earth at the spot where the temple now stands, where the sages had observed their penance to invoke Shiva.

Chidambaram comes from the old Tamil word *chith ambalam*, meaning 'mind's space'. Shiva, who was in the form of Nataraja, is said to have filled the sacred space with his dancing and the temple is also called Shiva's *sabha*, or concert stage.

All the gods, heavenly beings and otherworldly creatures gathered to watch him dance. To the beat of the *udukai*, a tiny drum, and the rhythm of his ankle bells, Nataraja danced, his feet moving lightning fast, his matted hair swirling around him, his eyes shimmering in bliss. This dance was frozen in time in the bronze sculpture that can be seen in the temple. The temple walls have horizontal panels filled with sculptures of dancers in various poses.

Nataraja dances within a circle of fire, which depicts the circle of life. The demon Mooka lies trampled beneath his right foot, symbolic of ignorance being destroyed by Nataraja.

This event of Nataraja's dance in Chidambaram is made immortal in the Tamil song *Natanam Adinar* (He Danced) in the raga Vasantha in Carnatic music, composed by the 19th-century poet Gopalakrishna Bharati.

Every year, in the months of February and March, the Chidambaram Natyanjali Festival is held. Bharatanatyam performers dance to this song, invoking the beauty and majesty of the original lord of dance.

Temples praised in songs

The Tamil phrase *paadal petra sthalam* refers to those temples and their deities that have been specially mentioned in the religious poetry by the Nayanmars and Alwars. Nayanmars wrote special hymns called *Thevaram* in praise of Shiva and his temples (like the Chidambaram Nataraja Temple). The Alwars wrote special songs called *Pasurams* in praise of Vishnu's 108 *divya desams* or sacred temples.

The Song of the Wood Spirits

Sri Durga Parameshwari Temple, Dakshina Kannada, Karnataka

The coastal districts of Karnataka, like Udupi and Dakshina Kannada, are dotted with many temples. They are famous for the many folk and ritual dance-dramas performed at the festivals that take place there from November to May.

The most famous among the song and dance rituals in Karnataka is the Yakshagana (the song of nature spirits). *Yaksha*s are spirits of the forests and woods, who create magic and mischief. Male dancers dress in elaborate costumes as demons or spirits, sporting colourful faces, garlands and costumes to dance to musical plays based on Hindu fables and myths around gods, goddesses and the deities of these temples.

While Yakshagana musical plays are held across many festivals and fairs, the one linked to the Sri Durga Parameshwari Temple at Kateel, standing in an islet in the middle of River Nandini, is particularly popular.

Once, when the world was suffering from a drought, the sage Jabali asked the divine cow, Kamadhenu, to feed the starving people. As Mother Kamadhenu was busy, she asked her daughter, Nandini, to go down to Earth instead.

Now, how many of us have been lazy when our parents asked us to run errands? Well, Nandini was too, and so the angry sage cursed her to flow like a river.

According to the Sri Durga Parameshwari Temple legend, the goddess Durga was asked to come down to Earth by Sage Jabali to kill an evil demon called Arunasura. When the goddess, in the form of Parameshwari, appeared on Earth, the demon attacked her with his sword. She quickly turned into a statue, and when Arunasura's sword hit the statue, a swarm of bees came forth and stung the demon to death.

The *ugra brahmari*, or queen bee, who attacked the demon was the goddess herself. After the battle, the devotees requested the angry goddess to offer her blessings in her *soumya roopa* (pleasant form), as she does in the temple.

The battle between Goddess Parameshwari and Arunasura took place in Kateel, located on River Nandini. Now, Kateel was freed from the demon's rule.

The Yakshagana performances in this temple are most well-loved among the people of Karnataka.

The Dancing Gems

Sri Govindajee Temple, Imphal, Manipur

The Manipuri dance is an elegant, lyrical art form, famous in eastern India. It is a temple art. It is said that the first Manipuri temple dancers were *gandharvas*, divine creatures who left behind this dance about the love of Radha and Krishna for human devotees. It was Usha, the goddess of dawn, who had taught this beautiful dance to the *gandharvas*.

The themes of these dance-dramas are stories from the *Puranas*, tales of Shiva and Parvati, and the famous *Raslila* (the joyful dance of Krishna and Radha with her friends). Instruments like cymbals and the *pung*, or drums, are used as musical accompaniments.

According to a temple legend, the 18th-century king Bhagya Chandra was a devotee of Lord Krishna. He once had a vision of Krishna asking him to build a temple and an idol made of wood from a jackfruit tree.

The king soon forgot about the dream as he got busy fighting his enemies, who finally captured him in battle.

The victorious army asked the king to tame an elephant and, if he could do so, he would be freed and given his kingdom back.

The frightened king could not sleep the night before the challenge. He prayed to Krishna for help, who appeared in his dream and asked him not to worry, but to stand before a jackfruit tree in the ground where he would face the elephant the next morning.

The next day as King Bhagya Chandra stood before a jackfruit tree, the angry elephant saw the form of Krishna in the tree. He bowed in prayer before the king, leaving those watching shocked.

King Bhagya Chandra was freed after this miracle, and he went back to his kingdom and built the temple, sculpting the idols from a jackfruit tree as promised to Krishna, his beloved Govindajee.

On a full moon night, the *Raslila* was performed at this temple as part of the inauguration ceremony. Since then, on special occasions like Janmashtami, Manipuri dances are performed in the temple.

The Big Deal about Dance

Brihadeshwara Temple, Thanjavur, Tamil Nadu

The Brihadeshwara temple in Thanjavur, Tamil Nadu, is where the dance steps of *sadir*, known today as

Bharatanatyam, were written, lessons were learnt and performed before the Chola emperor and the temple deity, Shiva, in his form as Brihadeshwara, or the Big One.

The Chola king was a devoted follower of Shiva. It is said that one night, Shiva appeared in Rajaraja's dream and told him to build a temple. The next morning, the king gave the order for the temple to be constructed. It would have to be massive, so as to demonstrate the might of the Chola Empire. The Shiva idol that would be enshrined in the temple also had to be gigantic.

The temple, called *Periya Kovil* in Tamil, or Big Temple, sprawls over 30,000 sq. feet and, inside the shrine, the Brihadeshwara lingam is 29 feet tall and 54 feet in circumference!

There is plenty of proof of the Big Temple's link with music and dance. The bottom walls and sides of the main temple building on the north side are covered by inscriptions in the Grantha and Tamil script.

The stone inscriptions list 400 dancing girls, 200 musicians, singers like oduvars (a community of readers of devotional hymns), and others who worked in the temple. Much like an attendance register, the inscriptions tell us about the many devadasis (special temple dancers), who performed the *sadir*. These temple dancers were also learned in the many forms of performance art; some were critics and some were even scholars. They received salaries in the form of land or grains from the king.

Besides this, over 80 classical dance poses listed in the *Natya Shastra* are sculpted on the upper-storey walls, corridors and columns!

Thanjavur is also known for its veena makers near the temple. The veena is the sacred stringed music instrument of Goddess Saraswati.

No other temple in India has such a close association with dance, music and the arts like the Big Temple, which is quite a big deal!

The Dance of the Gods

Muchilot Bhagavathy Temple, Kannur, Kerala

The jade-coloured hills of north Malabar in Kerala have temples that depict the magical and the mysterious through dance and song. Many of them host brilliant and spectacular performances of Theyyam, ritual occult dances, at open squares in the temple precincts or in the fairgrounds and woods called *kavu* near the temples.

Theyyam is a nearly 800-year-old dance form, which combines magical rituals and stories of gods, goddesses, demons and spirits and ancestor worship. It is derived from the Malayalam word *deivam* (god), and the audience believe that the spirit of the local god animates the dancer during his performance! The dances are set to feverish drum beats, using musical instruments and percussions like *chenda, kurumkuzhal* and *veekkuchenda.*

The male dancers wear decorative costumes, with huge headgear studded with adornments in fiery reds, blazing oranges and glittering gold and silver leaves. Their faces are painted crimson and marked with dots, their eyes and mouths elaborately embellished with curly twists, making them look fierce. And their skirts are elaborate, made of cloth or grass, with decorative trimmings.

Once, a young girl called Annapurneshwari lived in the beautiful region of north Malabar in Kerala. She had a strange aura around her, and some people believed that she had been blessed by Lord Shiva – that she was born of the divine beads of sweat that dotted his brow.

The village elders were jealous of Annapurneshwari's knowledge and her capacity to answer intelligently. They frequently held quizzes to test her. They were envious of her smartness, and they insulted and brought dishonour upon her.

Hurt and upset by their cruel words and insults to her intelligence, she decided to burn herself one day. But Shiva saved her life, and sent her back to this spot on Earth, now known as Kannur, to protect the world and cure it from fevers and pestilences.

The Theyyam performances at this temple are very famous and draw a number of spectators.

Swaying Dance

Thyagarajaswamy Temple, Tiruvarur, Tamil Nadu

Meet the god of sacrifice, who likes to sway to dance and music! The large temple deity at Tiruvarur is Thyagarajaswamy, or the lord who sacrifices worldly pleasures for ascetic penance.

Indra, the king of heavens, once decided to play a trick on the Chola emperor in Tiruvarur, a devotee of Shiva. The king had a dream about Shiva sitting and swaying in the lotus that floated from Vishnu's navel, where Brahma usually resided. Indra showed the king six replicas of the deities of Shiva and Vishnu in the same pose, but the king, whose eyes were filled with pure devotion, was able to spot the right one to be installed at the temple in Tiruvarur.

The other six deities were installed in other temples across the Cauvery delta. During special occasions, bearers carry the garlanded deity of Shiva on a palanquin and dance the *saptavidangami,* or seven steps of swaying, as they carry it. When devotees gather, it seems as though the deity itself is swaying.

The temple at Tiruvarur is also the holy place where famous south Indian classical music composers like Muthuswami Dikshitar, Syama Sastri and Saint Thyagaraja, who are named after the deities of this town, have composed many songs.

The Songs of the Sword of Vishnu

Balaji Venkateswara Temple, Tirupati, Andhra Pradesh

Hailed as the *Andhra Pada Pitamaha*, or the Grandfather of Telugu song writing, saint and composer Annamacharya was believed to have been born of Nandaka, the divine sword Lord Vishnu carried, a symbol of sharp intelligence and knowledge. A 15th-century musician, Annamacharya was a devotee of Venkateswara and composed thousands of songs in praise of him, which are sung even today. He called his devotional songs 'musical garlands' to adorn the deity of Venkateswara. His songs are like stories, of him chatting with, loving or even quarrelling with Vishnu. Many of his compositions are found as inscriptions on the walls of the Venkateswara Temple in Tirupati.

Divine Music

Panchanatheeshwara Temple, Thiruvaiyaru, Tamil Nadu

If there's a temple town famed in south India for music, it is Thiruvaiyaru, in the Cauvery delta basin, in Thanjavur district.

The Shiva deity in the temple is worshipped as Lord Panchanatheeswar, also called Ayyarappan or Lord of Five Rivers. Thiruvaiyaru (meaning, the sacred five rivers) gets its name from the rivers of the Cauvery delta: Cauvery, Kudamurutti, Vennar, Vettar and Vadavar.

In the 18th and 19th centuries, Thiruvaiyaru came under the spotlight because of Saint Thyagaraja, the most respected classical musician of Carnatic music in south India. While Thyagaraja is famed for his compositions in praise of Rama, he also composed songs praising the temple deity of Thiruvaiyaru, Ayyarappan.

On the banks of the river, every year, a famous musical festival called the Thyagaraja Aradhana Festival is held. Here, Carnatic musicians from all over the world gather to sing his devotional songs.

Thyagaraja is one of the three famous composers of Carnatic music. He along with Syama Sastri and Muthuswamy Dikshitar were called the 'Trinity of Carnatic Music'. A musical prodigy or genius since his childhood, he composed thousands of Bhakti or devotional songs that are sung even today among Carnatic music lovers.

The Lord with the Lotus Belly Button

Anantha Padmanabhaswamy Temple, Thiruvananthapuram, Kerala

The Anantha Padmanabhaswamy Temple was built in the 18th century by the maharaja of the kingdom of Travancore. The temple's deity is Lord Anantha Padmanabhaswamy (Vishnu who is *anantha*, or lying on a bed made by his snake). He is called Padmanabhaswamy, or Vishnu from whose navel rises a lotus where Brahma resides.

In the 19th century, the then king of Travancore was Maharaja Swathi Tirunal, who was a classical musician and singer of both Hindustani and Carnatic music. He composed hundreds of songs, and all his songs had the same musical *mudra*, or signature, hailing Padmanabha, the lord who reposes in the temple.

To cherish the musical memory of this extraordinary king, each year the Travancore royal family leads the famous musical festival called Swathi Sangeethotsavam at the Kuthira Maligai, a palace near the Padmanabhaswamy Temple.

Divine Wake-Up Songs

Andal Temple, Srivilliputhur, Tamil Nadu

Do you have problems waking up in the mornings before getting dressed to go to school?

Well, Lord Venkateshwara doesn't have this problem that we mere mortals have. Dawn, with its promise of a new day, is marked by the singing of the *Venkateshwara Suprabhatam.* These are verses believed to have been composed by Sage Vishwamitra to awaken his royal pupil, Rama, during his days as a student in his gurukul.

Vishnu's musical awakening during *Marghazi*, one of the most auspicious periods in the Tamil calendar, is truly special.

During *Brahma muhurtam*, or predawn, the lanes around Vishnu temples are filled with devotional singing. The walking group sings the *Thirupavai*, a set of 30 hymns called *Pasuram*, and *Nachiar Tirumozhi*, composed by the iconic Vishnu devotee, the poetess Andal. She is the only female saint and poetess among the pantheon of 12 saints of Vishnu in south India, the Alwars.

Singing the *Pasuram* is a unique kind of worship during this beautiful time of the year, when the sun is mellow and the early morning breeze is tender. Young women find these songs special for they are about the love and dreams that the saint Andal had for her wedding or divine union with Maha Vishnu.

In mythology, Srivilliputhur was called Varahakshetra, or the land of sweet-smelling *champaka* trees, and was ruled by a queen. Here, the sages Bhrigu and Markandeya were saved by Lord Vishnu from Kalanerai, a demon who troubled the sages and disturbed their worship. The queen's son Villi founded this city, after having a dream in which the lord directed him to build it.

Here lived the devotee, Periyalvar, a priest at the Vishnu temple in Srivilliputhur. One day, he found a beautiful baby girl under a tulsi plant inside the temple. A shrine marks this spot inside the temple today.

Periyalvar named the child Kothai, and she too grew to be a devotee of Lord Vishnu. Each morning, she would string a garland of tulsi flowers, wear it on her shoulders and admire it, before adorning the idol in the temple. Since she almost presided over the Vishnu deity in the temple with loving propriety, she was called Andal, or she who called the shots!

Dance like a Man!

Andal Temple, Srivilliputhur, Tamil Nadu

In some of the Vishnu temples in Tamil Nadu, male priests dance to divine music before the deity. This tradition is thousands of years old, and you can witness it if you visit the Andal Temple at Srivilliputhur, in Tamil Nadu.

It is called *Arayar Sevai*, the performance of the musical verses of *Nalayira Divya Prabhandham* (the 4,000 sacred hymns in praise of Vishnu) during the 21 days of the *Marghazhi* festival (December–January). The *Arayars* are male temple priests, believed to have been gifted the musical instruments of the cymbals and chimes by Lord Vishnu himself.

The first *Arayar* was Nathamuni, a scholar and a devotee of Lord Vishnu. He would chant these hymns in front of the shrine of the deity, to the rhythmic stamping of his feet, the bells on his ankles chiming in tune with the song. The dance steps would accompany the recital of divine tales from the *Nalayira Divya Prabhandam* about Andal, the beloved female saint of Lord Vishnu, the dance of Krishna slaying the evil demon Kamsa, Lord Rama's victory over Ravana and many others.

A family of priests, across many generations, have performed this temple ritual dance. The dancers wear long, white *dhoti*s with gold-trimmed borders wrapped around their hips. They also wear a conical silk hat, which is embroidered with Vishnu's symbols of the conch, discus, and the *namam*, a mark of Vishnu in white and red.

Abhangs for the Almighty

Sant Tukaram Maharaj Gatha Mandir, Dehu, Maharashtra

Poverty and pain drove Saint Tukaram to compose thousands of Bhakti songs. The proof of his musical expression is found in the Sant Tukaram Maharaj Gatha Mandir, where many of his *abhang*s, or short divine poems in the Marathi language, in praise of Lord Vithoba, are carved on the walls of the temple. They're set to music as kirtans, or devotional songs.

Tukaram's family were devotees of Lord Vithoba (a deity with the qualities of both Krishna and Vishnu).

Tuka, as he was fondly called, lived in a happy home when tragedy struck and he lost his parents. Later, his family life, with wife Rakhuma Bai and a son, was destroyed, when they starved to death during a horrible famine in the 17th century.

Deeply stirred by the pain and poverty around him, Tukaram became a wandering mendicant in the beautiful Sahyadri Hills in the Western Ghats, meditating and composing bhakti songs.

While there are several temples to mark Tukaram's birth and death in Dehu, the Sant Tukaram Maharaj Gatha Mandir is a huge structure with towers made of white marble. Its walls are carved with many *abhang*s that are sung as kirtans until today.

Tukaram's *abhang*s are almost conversations with god, written in simple language so everyone can understand them.

The Dance of Burden

Dhandayudhapani Temple, Palani, Tamil Nadu

Kavadiattam, or *Kavadi*, is a folk dance performed by devotees balancing a curved or semi-circular piece of wood on their shoulders. It is festooned with colourful ribbons, garlands and peacock feathers to make it look attractive.

Dancers perform before Muruga, with cries of '*Muruganukku arohara*' ('Oh Muruga, please lessen the burden I am suffering').

While Kavadi dances are performed across Tamil Nadu, Malaysia, Singapore and Sri Lanka, it all began in Palani.

One day, Lord Shiva called the sage Agastya and asked him to carry two hills, Shivagiri and Shaktigiri, to Earth and install them in a special spot. Agastya was a dwarf and found it difficult to balance the two hills, or *kavadi*s, on his shoulders. He asked the demon, Idumban, who was his disciple, to carry them down for him.

Idumban carried them for a long time, but the burden began hurting his shoulders. So he set the hills down, to take some rest. When he tried to lift the two hillocks again, he found that they were stuck and could not be moved.

As he struggled to lift the hills up, huffing and puffing, a beautiful boy appeared before him and told him to leave the hills be. Idumban was angered by this and started a fight. In the battle, he was crushed by the boy, who revealed himself as Muruga, the lord of the hills.

A defeated Idumban requested the god for a boon. He said all devotees who prayed to Muruga to lessen their burdens or sufferings will have to carry a *kavadi* on their shoulders up to all Muruga temples, asking for his blessings. The special songs composed in Tamil that accompany the dance-march are called *Kavadichindu*.

As you approach the Dhandayudhapani Temple on Palani Hill, there's a shrine dedicated to Idumban at the foothill to mark this story, and devotees dance as they go up the hill to the temple.

Play of Tales

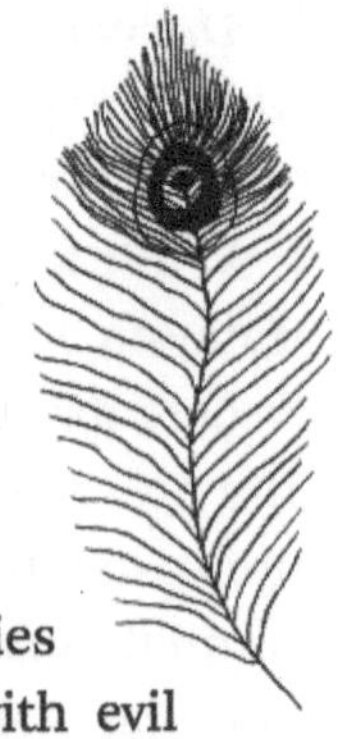

Sri Krishna Temple, Guruvayur, Kerala

The Sri Krishna Temple at Guruvayur is dedicated to Krishna's endearing avatar as a divine little boy. Each day, the Guruvayur Temple has a performance called Krishnattam, a traditional dance-drama based on the stories on Krishna's life: his boyhood, his fights with evil demons and many more. It is a brilliant sight as the dancers wear elaborate Kathakali costumes, colourful face paint and dazzling jewels.

There is a special story called *Krishnagiti* behind how these temple dances began. Once, the king of Kozhikode, Raja Manaveda, dreamt of receiving a bright peacock feather from Lord Krishna, who wears it on his crown. The king discussed his dream with the temple priest, who took King Manaveda to a grove of *elanji,* or bulletwood trees, and asked him to hide himself and watch, without making a sound.

As dawn broke, Krishna appeared in the form of a little boy and began dancing. The king could not contain himself, and rushed forward to hug and play with the cute child-god. However, as soon as he went close by, the child disappeared, leaving behind a peacock feather.

The king ordered that special plays be performed at the Guruvayur temple in praise of Lord Krishna after the miracle he had witnessed. As a symbol of the king's dream, Krishnattam dancers wear peacock feathers as part of their costume.

Krishnattam is based on the eight dramatic plays about Krishna's life and miracles. They are *Avataram* (birth of Krishna), *Kaliamardanam* (killing of the poisonous serpent Kalia), *Rasakrida* (dance of Krishna and *gopikas*), *Kamsavadham* (slaying of his uncle, the demon Kamsa), *Swayamvaram* (Krishna's wedding to Rukmini), *Banayuddham* (Krishna's battle with the demon Narakasuran), *Vividavadham* (Krishna's role in the Mahabharata), and *Swargaroham* (Krishna leaving Earth for Vaikunta or heaven).

In most temples, devotees offer fruits, milk or sweets to the deity, but at the temple of Guruvayur, devotees can choose to offer these dance-dramas! Every day, devotees pay and book various Krishnattam dances as offerings at the temple hall before a huge brass lamp burning bright, lighting these blessed performances.

Tansen's Musical Magic

Shiva Mandir, Behat, Gwalior, Madhya Pradesh

There was once a musical genius whose songs could bring rains, light lamps and even tame rogue elephants!

He was Tansen, often called the Father of Hindustani classical music. He was especially famous for the Gwalior *gharana*, named after the city where he lived as a musician. He was handpicked to join the court musicians of Emperor Akbar, who fondly called the bard Mian Tansen. Many ragas like *Mian ki Malhar* or *Mian ki Todi* are easy to identify as they carry the prefix of Tansen's title, *Mian*.

Tansen composed songs in praise of Shiva and Krishna, Ganesha and Saraswati in Sanskrit as well as Brajbhasa, so they could be sung and understood by royals and commoners alike.

Tansen was one of the *Navratna*, or the nine gems, of Emperor Akbar's court. When he died, the emperor had a special tomb built near the composer's Sufi guru's tomb in Gwalior.

Each year in December, the Tansen Samaroh festival is held. Musicians from all over India come together to participate in this festival.

There is a Shiva temple in a village called Behat, in Madhya Pradesh, which has a special connection with Tansen. According to folktales, Tansen's real name was Ramtanu Pandey, and he was a simple village boy. Each day, Ramtanu would offer goat milk to the Shiva deity in the temple and sing beautifully before it, as the villagers watched, charmed by his voice.

Legends say that the trees around the temple would stir by his singing and the walls of the temple swayed to the magic of his music. Apparently, that is why the shrine looks a little slanted. Tansen's divine music touched everyone – from villagers and emperors to even the walls of temples!

The Reptile's Raga

Sri Subrahmanya Temple, Peralassery, Kerala

In the Sri Subrahmanya Temple in Kannur, one can find an unusual form of song and dance as devotional expression. This art form is called *Pulluvan Paatu*, or the songs of the Pulluvar community, who are known to be serpent worshippers and bird hunters. They perform songs and dances to please the snake gods near forests and groves. There is a special raga called *Punnagavarali* that is said to mesmerize the snakes into swaying and dancing to it.

The Peralassery Subrahmanya Temple's main idol is a king cobra. Deities and idols of Subrahmanya, or Muruga, across temples have him with his mount, the peacock, which is often seen holding a writhing serpent in its beak or holding the snake down with its clawed feet. It is believed that the snake is a symbol of ego or arrogance that Muruga's peacock holds in check. Around this temple's compound, under the trees, are many stone idols of snakes, especially of king cobras, with their hoods raised. Devotees rub these idols with vermilion and turmeric, and place eggs as offerings before the shrine as it is believed that snakes like to eat eggs.

The town of Peralassery and its temple are also associated with the Ramayana. It is said that Rama and Lakshmana offered prayers here on their way to Lanka to bring Sita back. Rama removed a bangle from his wrist and placed it on the shrine, and began his worship to Subrahmanya, the god of war. *Per* means big and *ala* means bangle, after which the temple town is named.

The *Pulluvan Paatu* are performed before the temple on auspicious occasions by singers called *Nagampatikal*, or snake-song singers, to the accompaniment of folk instruments. The *Sarpamthullal*, or snake dance, said to evoke magic and the spirits, is also a ritual dance performed over geometric floor decorations called *kolam*.

Musical Pillars

Vijayavitthala Temple, Hampi, Karnataka

The beginnings of Carnatic music can be traced to Saint Purandaradasa. He was one of the main singers of the Bhakti period (8–17th century CE), a time when many composers wrote songs in praise of gods; songs that were both lyrical and soulful.

Purandaradasa was a rich merchant, who gave up all his wealth to be a *Haridasa* or a wandering devotee of Krishna or Vitthala. He settled down near Vijayanagaram, now called Hampi, with his wife and sons, and composed many devotional songs here.

Each morning, Purandaradasa would leave for the town, wearing a garland of tulsi leaves, that Vishnu wears, and bells on his ankles, singing songs in praise of Vitthala on his *tambura*, a stringed instrument.

On the banks of River Tungabhadra in Vijayanagaram lived a pious potter called Appana. Once, Purandaradasa went to his hut and heard Appana talking to Krishna inside his dark hut. He thought Appana was acting, and, in a fit of anger, struck him with a brick on his head, and left. All night, Purandaradasa could not sleep as he felt terrible about hitting the poor potter.

In the morning, he went to the temple and was shocked to see a bruise on the forehead of the temple idol. He ran back to Appana's hut and begged for forgiveness.

The Vitthala Temple in Hampi, on the banks of the Tungabhadra, is world famous for its architecture and is a heritage site. One of the striking features is the *ranga mantapa*, or carved pillared hall, whose pillars are said to make soft musical sounds when patted. Many people call them the 'Sa Re Ga Ma pillars' after the musical notes of Indian classical music.

The annual Purandaradasa Festival is held in the *ranga mantapa* in the winter where classical musicians come to perform.

Ye, People of Vishnu

Narsinh Mehta Choro, Gopinathji Temple, Junagadh, Gujarat

Gandhi's favourite song was 'Vaishnava Janato' (Ye, people of Vishnu), composed by none other than the 15th-century poet Narsinh Mehta, called the *Adikavi* (the forerunner among poets) of Gujarat.

Little Narsinh was pious and lived in Junagadh in Saurashtra. However, his childhood was beset by difficulties and tragedies. He could not speak until he was eight; he was orphaned at the age of five, and was brought up by his grandmother. His married life as a young man was also troublesome and one day, insulted at home by his in-laws, a hurt Narsinh left for a nearby forest and began to meditate.

Legends say that Narsinh was transformed by a vision of Krishna and Radha while meditating. He returned home to compose and sing over hundreds of kirtans in praise of Krishna.

Narsinh Mehta's Choro is a special place for devotees. It was where Narsinh held his devotional musical assemblies. A Gopinath temple dedicated to Krishna stands here now.

In the temple, there are shrines to the deity of Krishna, called Damodar here, and a shrine to Narsinh Mehta, Krishna's most special devotee, who composed timeless songs in his praise.

The Dance of the Mahanaris

Jagannath Temple, Puri, Odisha

Dance gurus say that watching an Odissi performance is like watching temple sculptures come to life. When you visit the Jagannath Temple in Puri, you can see for yourself how true this is. The panels of the temple are filled with sculptures of women dancing and striking poses, and they are so realistic, you can be fooled into thinking you are watching an Odissi performance!

The Odissi dance was born in the temples of Odisha. We can find early mentions of the dance in the list of rituals or special prayers for Lord Jagannath at the temple. The devadasis, or temple dancers, in Odisha were called *mahari* (a short form of *mahanari*, or special women). They lived in the temple precincts and performed as part of the daily devotional services, or *seva*. Various texts like the *Vishnu Purana*, *Srimad Bhagavatam* and *Vamadeva Samhita* mention Odissi dance and music as a ritual offering in the temple services.

The Mask of Devotion

Shiva Temple, Purulia, West Bengal

Did you know there is a world heritage list of dances and the Chhau dance is on it? Chhau is said to have military

origins, as a war dance, but is now popular as a festival folk dance performed by men.

Chhau is performed in West Bengal, Odisha and some districts of Bihar. The Chhau dances at the Sun Festival during the spring months (March–April) in West Bengal's Purulia district are very popular.

Chhau is also associated with the Gajan festival for Shiva. It is called *Shiber gajan,* which comes from *gar* and *jan*, or loud cries made by holy men who are Shiva bhakts. The festival marks Shiva's marriage to Harakali, an avatar of Devi, the mother goddess.

The Loharia Shiva Temple in Purulia is a famous pilgrimage site with fairgrounds for pilgrims to gather for festivities.

Chhau is performed on the ground and not on stages. The performances begin at night, by dinner time, and go on past midnight.

Chhau comes from the word *chaya*, or mask. In this dance form, male dancers wear elaborate masks with frightful expressions and enormous, colourful headgear. These masks are made by craftsmen from a village called Charida in Purulia. Made of paper, glue and bright shiny paints, these masks are decorated with glimmering blades of gold foil that twinkle in the light.

They dance to the tales from the Ramayana and the Mahabharata, Shiva and Shakti legends, set to the beats of the *dhol* and *damsa*, or kettle drums. Gods, demons, animals, birds are all popular characters in a Chhau dance performance.

Rustic pipe instruments accompany this mesmerizing dance form. The music is set to mark the speed and tempo, as the dancers often run onto the performing areas crying '*Cho, cho*!' to announce their arrival. The dance is marked by acrobatic jumping, called *ulfa*, which is thrilling to watch, and vigorous body movements.

Bison Horn Dance

Danteswari Mandir, Dantewada, Chhattisgarh

Once, Daksha, Shiva's father-in-law, decided to hold a special yagna, in his palace. He invited all the gods, heavenly creatures and, of course, his entire family. The only people he left out of the invitee list were his daughter Sati and her husband, Shiva.

You see, Daksha wasn't fond of his odd son-in-law, who was always covered in ashes, looked so fierce, and had *bhoota ganas* (think of them as hobgoblins) as his companions.

Sati was so angry with her father for not having invited her and Shiva to the yagna that she stormed into his palace on the day of the ritual and set herself on fire. An angry and distraught Shiva carried her dead body in his arms and danced the *tandav*, or the dance of destruction. So vigorous was his dance that the goddess's body parts went flying around and fell on various spots on the Earth. Each spot where her body fell is called a *Shaktipeetha* (the holy spot of Shakti).

It is said that one of the goddess's teeth (or *dant*) fell into the dense jungles of Bastar. Now there is a little town in the region called Dantewada, known for its Danteshwari Mandir. Here, during Dussehra, when Goddess Shakti is said to have killed the evil demon Mahishasura, a special dance performance is held as part of the celebrations.

This performance is called the Bison Horn dance, and it is performed by the Muria tribals of Bastar. Male dancers wear elaborate headgear made of bison horns and cowrie shells, while women wear red saris and use staffs to stamp the ground to the beat of drums.

The Queen of Songs

Meera Bai Kumbha Shyam Temple, Chittorgarh, Rajasthan

Some people follow their passion with great determination. Even when others try to stop them, they remain devoted to their cause.

Meera, a princess of the Mewar royal family born in the 15th century in Rajasthan, was one such person.

When Meera was a little girl, a holy man visited her grandparents' home. He gave Meera a small idol of Krishna which she loved so dearly that she always carried it with her.

It was unusual for women from aristocratic families to rebel and abandon the wealthy life of the nobles and their married homes in search of divine love. But Meera did just that for Krishna!

That did not go down well with Meera's husband and family, who definitely did not like her wandering around like a mendicant, strumming her *tambura*, and singing songs in Krishna's name.

Folktales recount how her family tried to kill her on many occasions. However, she was miraculously saved by Krishna's divine grace each time.

'What do you do with a girl like Meera?' asked the shocked elders.

'Let's stop her singing,' said someone wickedly.

One day, Meera was chanting Krishna's numerous names when a basket of poisonous snakes was delivered to her by the palace guards. Meera, still humming, opened the lid of the basket, only to find coils and coils of fragrant garlands!

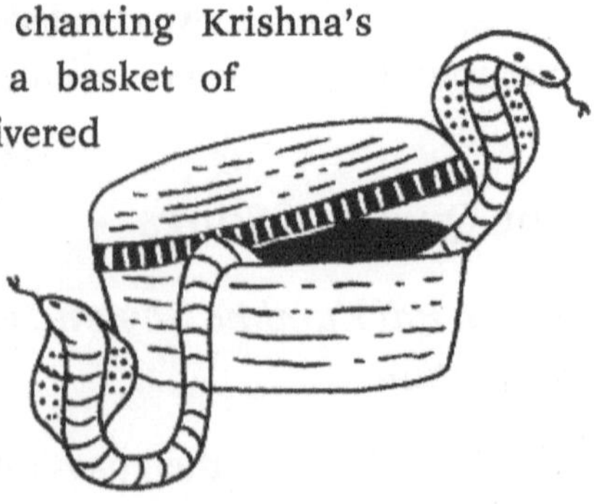

Another time, an evil aunt forced her to drink a cup of poison, but murmuring Krishna's name on her lips, Meera took a big gulp and the astonished aunt found that it had no effect on her!

Meera's songs in praise of Krishna are called Meera bhajans, sung in Rajasthani and Brajbhasa, and they remain popular to this date. They use delightful metaphors of birds, animals and nature to describe her state of mind or love for Krishna.

The Kumbha Shyam Temple at Chittorgarh is dedicated to various gods and goddesses. Inside it is the Meera Temple, which is dedicated to *her*. It has images of Krishna and paintings of Meera offering prayers to Krishna.

The Blind Bard

Shrinathji Temple, Govardhan, Uttar Pradesh

Surdas was a 16th-century composer, whose songs are sung even today. He was born blind into a poor family near Govardhan, the place of Krishna's childhood. The blind boy was a great devotee of Krishna. He would spend his time on the banks of River Yamuna, reciting Krishna's many different names.

One day, he left home and reached the town of Vrindavan, where the sounds and songs of Krishna, Radha and the *gopis* filled him with unbelievable devotion and happiness, and he stayed there for many years, composing songs in Krishna's name.

One legend has it that Krishna took the form of the divine boy Gopal once, and came down to Earth and sat before Surdas and listened to him sing in a garden bursting with flowers. Blind as he was, Surdas had no inkling of Gopal sitting before him, and sang so lovingly that the god was moved.

Surdas's devotional poetry and songs attracted many devotees. He was even appointed as the bard of the Shrinathji Temple in Govardhan.

According to a folktale, one morning Surdas and other devotees were seated before the shrine, waiting for the morning prayers at the temple. The priests had drawn the velvet curtain over the sanctum while they dressed the deity for the ritual. Bystanders noticed Surdas singing about the beauty of the lord and describing in great detail the decorations of Shrinathji. When the priests drew open the curtain, the devotees gathered in the temple were astonished to see that the blind Surdas had correctly described the deity's adornments to the last detail!

Surdas's bhajans and kirtans are sung on special festive occasions at the temple even today.

Rama's Lila

Sankat Mochan Temple, Varanasi, Uttar Pradesh

The *Ramlila*, or the musical drama presenting tales from the Ramayana, is a special performance in many towns across north India during Navratri and Ram Navami celebrations. While there are many versions of the Ramayana, the most popular one is Tulsidas's *Ramcharitmanas*, the story of Rama written in the Awadhi language. Many believe that Tulsidas was an incarnation of the divine poet Valmiki himself.

The 16th-century Bhakti poet was a resident of Varanasi, and was often found on the banks of River Ganga. The Tulsi

Ghat in Varanasi is named after him. He is said to have composed the first *Ramlila*.

Tulsidas once had a vision of Lord Hanuman blessing him. That spot is where the Sankat Mochan Temple now stands. Tulsidas founded the temple and composed the *Hanuman Chalisa*, 40 oral verses in praise of Lord Hanuman.

The Sankat Mochan Temple hosts a music and dance festival each year in April – attracting performers from across the country – where the divine poet Tulsidas's devotion once moved the gods themselves.

The Dance of Lights

Ganga Aarti, Varanasi, Uttar Pradesh

In Varanasi, India's oldest and holiest city, the River Ganga is also worshipped as the wife of Vishwanath, the city's presiding deity. Every evening, the ritual worship of *aarti*, or flames dancing on elaborate brass lamps, by priests to chants makes for a special kind of performance.

Along the river, there are banks called ghats. The ghats are marked by wide stone steps that lead to the river. There are 88 ghats along the river, and the most famous one is the Dashashwamedha Ghat, near the Vishwanath Temple. Legend has it that the ghat was first built by Brahma, who offered ten horses at a yagna to welcome Shiva into the city.

This ghat is where the *agni puja*, or worship with flames, is held. As dusk spreads over the sacred river, devotees gather here to witness a unique puja called the Ganga *aarti.* It is a spectacular sight – the dancing flames and the clouds of smoke from the incense sticks swirling around to the fierce beating of drums and chimes of cymbals, as the priests twirl the lit lamps in the growing darkness.

SELECT BIBLIOGRAPHY

Mythology: Timeless Tales of Gods and Heroes, 75th Anniversary Illustrated Edition by Edith Hamilton, Black Dog & Leventhal Publishers Inc., 2017

Hindu Myths by Wendy Doniger, Penguin India, 2005

Classical Hindu Mythology: A Reader in the Sanskrit Puranas by Cornelia Dimmitt, Temple University Press, 1978

The Complete World of Greek Mythology by R.G.A. Buxton, Thames & Hudson, 2004

Prasadam: Food of the Hindu Gods by Nalini Rajan, Vakils, Feffer and Simons Pvt Ltd, 2003

Bhog: Temple Food of India by Arun Budhiraja and Geeta Budhiraja, Krishna Prerna Charitable Trust, 2012

Sacred Groves of India – A Compendium by Nanditha Krishna and M. Amirthalingam, CPR Environmental Education Centre, 2014

Sacred Plants of India by Nanditha Krishna and M Amirthalingam, Penguin India, 2016

http://www.indiaenvironmentportal.org.in

shodhganga.inflibnet.ac.in

biodivvy.com/2017/11/14/lessons-from-the-sacred-groves-of-india

Temples of India – Abode of the Divine by Tarun Chopra, Navyug Publishers, 2016

Temples in India: Origin and Developmental Stages by S. Vijayakumar, S.P. Gupta, DK Printworld (P) Ltd, 2010

A History of South India: From Prehistoric Times to the Fall of Vijayanagar by KA Nilakanta Sastri, R Champakalakshmi, Oxford Publications, 1997

Elements of Indian Art: Including Temple Architecture, Iconography and Iconometry by S.P. Gupta, DK Print World Ltd, 2006

World Heritage Series – Great Living Chola Temples by Dr C. Chandramouli, Tamil Nadu Tourism, 2008

108 Vishnu Temples: Architectural Splendour, Spiritual Bliss by Avey Varghese, Niyogi, 2016

Indian Temple Sculpture by John Guy, Victoria & Albert Museum, 2018

Indian Sculpture: Towards the Rebirth of Aesthetics by Carnel Berkson, Abhinav Publications, 2009

The Koyil Olugu: History of the Srirangam Temple by T.S. Parthasarathy, Tirumala Tirupati Devasthanam, 1954

Krishna: Srimad Bhagavata Purana by Edwin Bryant, Penguin, 2004

Thiruvilaiyadal Puranam by R. Ponnammal, Giri Trading Agency Pvt Ltd, 2013

The First Spring – The Golden Age of India by Abraham Eraly, Penguin, 2011

Shrinathji: Pichwais: The Manifestation of Pushtimarg by Anu Julka, Patridge Publishing India, 2014

https://www.livemint.com/Sundayapp/5baXWamO6RTLyc2gWiBCPP/Udupi-the-preamble.html

Classical Music of India: A Practical Guide by Lakshminarayana Subramaniam, Viji Subramaniam, Tranquebar Press, 2018

The Devotional Poems of Mirabai: Esctatic Poems by Robert Bly and Jane Hirshfield, Beacon Press, 2004

The Dance of Siva: Essays on Indian Art and Culture by Ananda K. Coomaraswamy, Dover Publications Inc., 2003

ACKNOWLEDGEMENTS

Thanks to this book I have learnt not to underestimate the good results that a bunch of quizzing nerds and a big bowl of crisps can bring about.

Thanks to Gitanjali Lal for the above.

Much thanks to my patient, calm and incisive editor, Nimmy Chacko, who allowed a chat over an apple cake and a pot of tea to turn into this book; Jyotsna Raman, for her meticulous copy-editing, and Niyati Dhuldhoya for her eagle-eyed proofreading.

Thanks to Sharanya Kunnath for her imaginative illustrations in this book.

To my sister Sujatha Sridharan and my niece Anjana Sridharan for their sharp reading of the book's draft and precise comments.

Endless thanks to Janaki Venkataraman for taking time to read the first drafts and for much more than words can say.

Thanks to Padmaja Venket Ram, pal, patron, pillar for her encouragement for all my crazy schemes since we were kids.

A bear hug to young Aryamaan Sen for showing care and support while writing this book.

Fist bump to Supriya Sehgal for goading me on when I worried.

Sunanda Biswas, for showing me a kind heart is truly divine.

Much love to Soutik Biswas, the non-believer who believed in me to complete this.

And thank god for the many colourful stories that have been passed on to me by friends, family and teachers.